MW01102669

How to Be a
Co-worker and an Elder

and How to Fulfill Their Obligations

Witness Lee

Living Stream Ministry
Anaheim, CA • www.lsm.org

© 1996 Living Stream Ministry

First Edition, November 1996.

ISBN 978-1-57593-805-9

Published by

Living Stream Ministry
2431 W. La Palma Ave., Anaheim, CA 92801 U.S.A.
P. O. Box 2121, Anaheim, CA 92814 U.S.A.

Printed in the United States of America

15   16   17   18   19   /   12   11   10   9   8   7

CONTENTS

PREFACE

This book is a translation of messages given in Chinese by Brother Witness Lee in Anaheim, California in an international co-workers and elders' conference on October 1-3, 1996.

CHAPTER ONE

HOW TO BE A CO-WORKER AND AN ELDER

(1)

OUTLINE

I. To know Christ (Phil. 3:10), to particularly know that:
  A. He is both God and man.
  B. He possesses both divinity and humanity.
  C. In His humanity He accomplished His judicial redemption through His death.
  D. In His divinity He is carrying out His organic salvation in His resurrection.

II. To experience and enjoy Christ (to gain Christ—Phil. 3:8) in His full ministry in His three divine and mystical stages:
  A. In the first stage, the stage of His incarnation, from His human birth to His death:
    1. To bring the infinite God into the finite man.
    2. To unite and mingle the Triune God with the tripartite man.
    3. To express in His humanity the bountiful God in His rich attributes through His aromatic virtues:
      a. Christ expressed the bountiful God in His human living.
      b. Mainly expressing God in His rich attributes, that is, in the unsearchable riches of what God is.
      c. Through Christ's aromatic virtues by which He attracted and captivated people:
        1) Not by living His human life in the flesh.

        2) But by living His divine life in resurrection.

    4. To accomplish His all-inclusive judicial redemption:

       a. Terminating all things of the old creation.

       b. Redeeming all the things created by God and fallen in sin—Heb. 2:9; Col. 1:20.

       c. Creating (conceiving) the new man with His divine element—Eph. 2:15.

       d. Releasing His divine life from the shell of His humanity—John 12:24.

       e. Laying a foundation for His organic salvation and setting up the procedure to attain His ministry in the stage of His inclusion.

Prayer: Lord, thank You for putting us in Your recovery to be the slaves of Your children. As co-workers and elders we all are slaves in Your house. Lord, only You are the Lord, the Sovereign Master; we worship You, serve You, preach You, and dispense You to people. For Your sake we are willing to be Your household slaves to serve You and take care of Your children. O Lord, do speak a clear word to us again in these six meetings; speak something which You have not spoken before and which we have not heard before. It seems that we heard many things before but did not take them in. O Lord, we pray that You would give us a glorious beginning; glorify Yourself, glorify the Father, and glorify the Spirit. O Lord, we are Your slaves, and we can only bow down and worship before You, looking to You to grant us a good beginning.

O Lord, we also cannot forget Your enemy. While You are giving grace to us, he is disturbing us. Lord, we truly hate the evil one; we accuse him before You. We declare before You that You have already destroyed him through Your death in the flesh on the cross. We pray that You would destroy Your enemy, Satan, the evil one, among us in Your recovery. Lord, release Your children, release Your rich grace, and release Yourself that we may receive Your rich and abounding supply. Amen.

In this conference we want to see how to be a co-worker and an elder and how to fulfill the obligations of the co-workers and elders. The central burden of these messages can be expressed in the following statements:

(1) The full ministry of Christ is carried out in three stages for the fulfillment of God's eternal economy.

(2) In the first stage of incarnation to bring God into man, to express God in humanity, and to accomplish His judicial redemption.

(3) In the second stage of inclusion to be begotten as God's firstborn Son, to become the life-giving Spirit, and to regenerate the believers for His Body.

(4) In the third stage of intensification to intensify His organic salvation, to produce the overcomers, and to consummate the New Jerusalem.

This is a special conference originally initiated by the brothers from Taiwan. Since I have not returned to Taiwan for many years, they requested repeatedly that I speak in Chinese in this conference. In the past few years I did not comply since there should be no differences of nationalities in the Lord's recovery. Although we still have the language problem passed on to us from Babel, we keep the Lord's word by not having national differences. In the Lord's Body there is no room for any nation or race, but He is all. In the new man there is only our Lord, who is all the members and in all the members as their content. Since the Lord is in us, we should not have any national differences. Nevertheless, because we are still in our flesh, language remains a big problem. Hence, although we are releasing the messages in Chinese, may there be no differences of nationalities among us.

NOT ASSUMING A STATUS BUT
SERVING AS SLAVES

I want to speak a frank word to all of you. According to my many years of observation, the biggest problem with the co-workers and the elders is that many of them overly regard their status as a co-worker or an elder. Actually, as co-workers and elders, we have no status. According to God's love and grace, we are all His children and are of the same species as He. In this sense, we cannot say that we have no status. Our status is that we are God's species and God's children. According to His economy, out of His created and redeemed human race on the earth, God wants to gain the church, which is the Body of Christ, and, eventually, to have the New Jerusalem for the accomplishment of His eternal economy. In the process, there is a great deal of work and service, so there is the need to have co-workers and elders.

In the Gospels we can see clearly that Peter, James, and John were the first ones to follow the Lord. They were by the Lord's side following Him for three and a half years. At the end, the Lord brought them with Him to Jerusalem. He was going there to die for the accomplishment of God's economy, yet His followers were arguing on the way about which of them was the greatest (Mark 9:34; Luke 22:24). That was truly something ugly and shameful. They had followed the Lord for three and a half years; they had been beside Him and had received numerous revelations from Him. Then on their way to Jerusalem, the Lord told them repeatedly that He was going up to Jerusalem to die and on the third day He would be resurrected (Matt. 16:21; 17:22-23; 20:17-19). Although they heard the Lord saying that He was going to die, they did not hear Him saying that on the third day He would be resurrected. *Resurrection* was a foreign word incomprehensible to them.

They heard the word that the Lord was going to die, and they were also about to enter Jerusalem. Yet they were by the Lord's side arguing about who was the greatest among them. James and John were the Lord's cousins in the flesh, for their mother was the sister of Mary, the mother of the Lord Jesus. Hence, they asked their mother to pay a visit to the Lord Jesus, and she went and asked the Lord, "Say that these two sons of mine will sit, one on Your right and one on Your left, in Your kingdom." When the other ten disciples heard this, they were indignant concerning the two brothers (Matt. 20:20-24). James and John's bringing in their family relationship with the Lord was truly an ugly matter.

Then the Lord Jesus called the disciples to Him and said, "Whoever wants to become great among you shall be your servant, and whoever wants to be first among you shall be your slave" (vv. 26b-27). *Slave* here does not refer to a hired servant but to a purchased slave. According to Roman law, slaves had no human rights.

As co-workers and elders we are such slaves. Paul said, "For we do not preach ourselves but Christ Jesus as Lord, and ourselves as your slaves for Jesus' sake" (2 Cor. 4:5). This means that the believers were not to regard Paul, Peter, and others too highly simply because they were apostles and evangelists. Actually, they were the believers' slaves. Today we also should not regard ourselves as co-workers and elders; rather, we should consider ourselves as slaves of all people to serve all people.

My greatest burden is this: I hope that the Lord will give you mercy through my fellowship in love so that you all will be convinced and realize that to be a co-worker or an elder is to be a slave. Concerning this matter, the Lord Jesus set up a good example for us. He was the Lord and the Teacher, yet He emptied Himself and girded His loins to wash His disciples' feet, serving them as a slave (John 13:3-5). The Lord also commanded us to do as He did (vv. 12-17). We brothers who are co-workers and elders have been wrong, and we all have to repent. I say this with a painful heart because we always assume the position of being above others and do not allow others to say that we are wrong. If anyone says that we are wrong, we carry a grudge in our heart. This is not the proper attitude of a slave.

For this reason, first, we want to fellowship concerning how to be a co-worker and an elder. We must know that to be the children of God does not require learning. After our regeneration, spontaneously we became God's children, and for this we thank and praise the Lord. However, no one is a co-worker as soon as he is saved, and no one is an elder as soon as he is regenerated. To be a co-worker and an elder requires learning.

I. TO KNOW CHRIST

To be a co-worker or an elder, first, we must know Christ. In Philippians 3:10 Paul spoke about knowing Christ and the power of His resurrection and the fellowship of His sufferings, being conformed to His death. To know Christ is not a simple matter. I want to fellowship with you concerning how to know Christ mainly in four items. The co-workers and elders must know these items. Not only must you know them, but also you must know them thoroughly and be able to speak them to others. To know Christ is not to know Him in a common way but to know Him in a particular way. The riches of what Christ is, are unsearchable (Eph. 3:8), but among them, there are the four following items which we need to know in particular.

A. He Is Both God and Man

First, we must know particularly that Christ is both God and man. We should not think that we already know this. We need to be reminded again and again that Christ is both God and man. He was God and He became man, so He is both God and man. Thus, He is a God-man.

B. He Possesses Both Divinity and Humanity

Second, we need to know that since Christ is a God-man, He possesses both divinity and humanity. Some may say, "We also know this already." Maybe we know, but we do not know how to speak it. Concerning the divinity and humanity of Christ, we must have a thorough knowledge.

C. In His Humanity He Accomplished His Judicial Redemption through His Death

Third, we have to know that in His humanity Christ accomplished His judicial redemption through His death. To know Christ, we have to discern clearly that His being in His humanity is one thing and His being in His divinity is another thing. Concerning the redemption of Christ, the general saying is that Christ was a man with blood and flesh, so He could die for us in His flesh. The deeper way, however, is to say that Christ accomplished redemption in His humanity. We should not remain only in the general saying; this is an indication that our knowledge concerning Christ is not deep enough. We must penetrate the deepest part of the divine truth to see the intrinsic significance of Christ in His humanity.

In His humanity Christ accomplished redemption through His death. Christ had to die in order to fulfill God's judicial requirement (Heb. 9:22). Therefore, Christ's redemption is a judicial redemption, and it was accomplished in His humanity through His death according to God's judicial requirement, that is, according to the requirement of God's righteous law.

D. In His Divinity He Is Carrying Out His Organic Salvation in His Resurrection

Fourth, we also need to know that in His divinity Christ is carrying out His organic salvation in His resurrection. We need to see further that Christ's redemption is different from His salvation. Romans 5:10a says that we "were reconciled to God through the death of His Son"; this refers to His redemption. Romans 5:10b says, "Much more we will be saved in His life"; this refers to His salvation. The organic salvation is being carried out in resurrection by Christ in His divinity. This is new light and the new language given to us by God. In His divinity and in His resurrection, He is carrying out His organic salvation in the believers. The judicial redemption has been accomplished, but the organic salvation is being carried out.

We need to have a clear knowledge concerning these four items. Then whether we are co-workers or elders, when we go to shepherd and teach people, we can speak these things to them in a very clear way. The co-workers and elders need to know Christ particularly in these four main items. You must not despise these four items. You may think that you already know these things, but when you go to speak to others, you may not know how to do it or how to call their attention to the main points. This requires practice. The churches in Taiwan are presently practicing four things: praying, studying, reciting, and speaking. This is the right way. Every co-worker and elder must deal with these four items concerning Christ by pray-reading over them, studying them deeply, reciting them from memory, and speaking them thoroughly to present clearly the main points to others.

II. TO EXPERIENCE AND ENJOY CHRIST (TO GAIN CHRIST) IN HIS FULL MINISTRY IN HIS THREE DIVINE AND MYSTICAL STAGES

To be a co-worker or an elder, we also need to experience and enjoy Christ (to gain Christ—Phil. 3:8) in His full ministry in His three divine and mystical stages. How can we be a co-worker and an elder? First, we need to know Christ; second, we need to experience and enjoy Christ, that is, to gain Christ, in His full ministry. First, we have the knowledge, and then we have the experience and enjoyment. To experience and enjoy Christ is to gain Christ. In Philippians 3:8 Paul said, "...Christ Jesus my Lord, on account of whom I have suffered the loss of all things and count them as refuse that I may gain Christ." To "have" is not sufficient; we need to "gain." To gain Christ requires paying a price. To gain Christ is to experience, enjoy, and take possession of all His unsearchable riches by paying a price. This is not so simple. Hence, Paul went on to say, "Not that I have already obtained or am already perfected, but

I pursue....I do not account of myself to have laid hold; but one thing I do: Forgetting the things which are behind and stretching forward to the things which are before, I pursue toward the goal" (vv. 12-14a). It is not easy to win a game, and it is also not easy to win the victory in a war. These require us to pursue by forgetting the things which are behind and stretching forward to the things which are before. Likewise, we need to gain Christ by experiencing and enjoying Him in His full ministry.

A. In the First Stage, the Stage of His Incarnation, from His Human Birth to His Death

The full ministry of Christ is in three divine and mystical stages. The first stage, the stage of His incarnation, began with His human birth and ended with His death, including the entire course of His human life. Hence, His human birth, His passing through human living, and His death formed the stage of His incarnation.

1. To Bring the Infinite God into the Finite Man

In His full ministry in the first stage, the stage of His incarnation, Christ brought the infinite God into the finite man. Some may think that this point is very simple. However, perhaps the most you can say is that Christ in His incarnation brought "God into man"; you cannot say that He brought "the infinite God into the finite man." This is our new language today. God is infinite, and we human beings are finite. In His full ministry in the stage of His incarnation, Christ brought the infinite God into the finite man. One is infinite and the other is finite—how could the two become one? Nevertheless, it was carried out by Christ in His ministry. This is truly wonderful.

In general, most Christians today know only about the so-called Christmas to celebrate the birth of Christ as our Savior. However, they have not seen anything concerning the mystical aspect of the full ministry of Christ in the stage of His incarnation. I am very concerned and afraid that perhaps many co-workers and elders in the Lord's recovery have not entered into these deep and profound significances. Because of this, people find nothing interesting in the things which you speak, and they consider them something trite, something which even non-Christians have already heard. However, if you use the new language to speak the things seen in the new culture, telling people that, in His full ministry in the stage of His incarnation, Christ brought the infinite God into the finite man, people will be stirred up and will be interested in listening to you, because this is something not found in the old culture but in the new culture in the divine and mystical realm.

2. To Unite and Mingle the Triune God with the Tripartite Man

In His full ministry in the first stage of His incarnation, Christ also united and mingled the Triune God with the tripartite man. The Triune God is mysterious, and the tripartite man is difficult to understand. If we simply say that Christ united and mingled God with man, this is easy. However, according to the new language of the new culture in the divine and mystical realm, we need to say that Christ united and mingled the Triune God with the tripartite man. Concerning the Triune God, the Father is the source, the Son is the expression, and the Spirit is the entering in. Concerning the tripartite man, the spirit is the innermost part, the soul is in the middle, and the body is on the outside. This is not easy to explain clearly. Nevertheless, we need to know these things. If we do not have the knowledge, we cannot have the experience or the enjoyment. If we do not have the experience and enjoyment of Christ, we simply cannot gain Christ. Then when we go to speak to others, we will have nothing to say and will be poor in utterance and void of words. Even if we compel ourselves to speak, what we speak will be shallow, simple, and trite.

Some co-workers and elders often would say to me, "I don't dare to speak about these high truths because the believers whom I am serving cannot understand them according to their present spiritual condition." My reply is: "It is not that they cannot understand, but it is that you cannot speak clearly." It is only after we have known, experienced, and gained Christ that we can speak to others, according to the new language in the Lord's recovery, concerning this Christ whom we have gained. We must learn to use the new language to speak the new culture in the divine and mystical realm. Then people will listen to us with great pleasure and will definitely understand the things we speak. It is only by this way that we are qualified to be co-workers and elders. Otherwise, we are outdated in the Lord's move in the present age.

The ministry of Christ was not only to unite but even more to mingle the Triune God with the tripartite man. We must be able to tell people clearly what it means to be united and what it means to be mingled. When two pieces of wood are connected together, they are united; when two things are ground into powder and blended together, they are mingled. It is easy to speak concerning the union of God with man, but it is not easy to speak concerning the mingling of God with man. When we preach these truths, we need to explain them in detail.

3. To Express in His Humanity
the Bountiful God in His Rich Attributes
through His Aromatic Virtues

In His full ministry in the first stage of His incarnation, Christ also expressed in His humanity the bountiful God in His rich attributes through His aromatic virtues. No one can deny that the human virtues of Christ were aromatic; even when non-Christians read the four Gospels, they sense that the Jesus recorded in these books was a sweet and fragrant One, whose virtues were aromatic. This is because He expressed in His humanity the bountiful God in His rich attributes.

Our attributes are the characteristics of what we are. For example, losing one's temper easily, loving to speak first, speaking carelessly and irresponsibly, and acting lightly are human attributes. On the other hand, behaving cautiously, speaking rationally, doing things purposefully, and not acting irresponsibly or carelessly are also human attributes. Our God has His attributes, and His attributes are rich because He is great and bountiful. He is love, light, holiness, and righteousness. These rich attributes were expressed by the Lord Jesus in His humanity to become the aromatic virtues in His humanity.

The record in the four Gospels shows that when some people brought their little children to Jesus that He might lay His hands on them and pray, they were rebuked by the disciples. But Jesus said, "Allow the little children and do not prevent them from coming to Me, for of such is the kingdom of the heavens" (Matt. 19:13-15). The Lord's way was different from the disciples' way. The disciples did not act in accordance with God's attributes. God has chosen the foolish, the weak, the lowborn, and the despised of the world (1 Cor. 1:27-28); throughout the generations according to His love, forbearance, and forgiving grace, He has called, one by one, those who are weak and have nothing, who are like the little children. In this way Christ expressed God's attributes in His humanity.

God is bountiful; hence, He is rich in His attributes, His characteristics. Only some of the rich attributes of the bountiful God were lived out by the Lord on the earth in His humanity and seen by men as the virtues expressed in His humanity, yet these virtues were so aromatic and sweet. In His human living Christ expressed the bountiful God mainly in His rich attributes, that is, in the unsearchable riches of what God is.

Furthermore, Christ in His humanity expressed God through His aromatic virtues by which He attracted and captivated people. The record in Matthew 4 shows us that when the Lord Jesus was walking beside the Sea of Galilee, He saw Peter, John, and James, who were either fishing or mending nets with their fathers. Then He called them, saying, "Come after Me." Immediately they followed Him, giving up their net mending, abandoning their boats, and forsaking their father (vv. 18-22). To this day I still do not understand why it is that when He simply said, "Come after Me," the disciples forsook everything to follow Him. I truly believe that at that time the Lord Jesus must have displayed an aromatic power in His countenance and His voice which could really attract and captivate people.

To be attracted and captivated is to be charmed. People often asked us, "Who has captivated you? Wake up!" Once we are charmed by the Lord, we are charmed forever, so it is difficult for us to be awakened. This may be illustrated by a male and a female falling in love at first sight; the male is charmed by the female, and the female is attracted and captivated by the male. Likewise, the Lord must have had an indescribable sweetness and aroma emanating from Him in His humanity. If we had been with the Lord at that time, we also would have been "foolishly" charmed by Him.

Peter was charmed by the Lord to such an extent that although he was rebuked by the Lord frequently, he still determined to follow Him. The Lord's frequent rebuking could not make him go away. Today I dare not speak strong words to the co-workers and elders. If my rebuke is strong, I am afraid that they will not be able to take it and will quit. However, Peter was thick-skinned. He had been rebuked by the Lord many times, but he still followed Him. On the night of His betrayal, the Lord said to the disciples, "You will all be stumbled because of Me this night." Then Peter answered and said to Him, "If all will be stumbled because of You, I will never be stumbled" (Matt. 26:31-33). And the Lord said to him, "Simon, Simon, behold, Satan has asked to have you all to sift you as wheat. But I have made petition concerning you that your faith would not fail." Peter said, "Lord, I am ready to go with You both to prison and to death." But the Lord said, "I tell you, Peter, a rooster will not crow today until you deny three times that you know Me" (Luke 22:31-34). Not only did Peter disbelieve this word, but he even said, "Even if I must die with You, I will by no means deny You" (Matt. 26:35). Later, while Peter was sitting in the courtyard of the high priest, a little servant girl came to question him. Because of her questioning, Peter denied the Lord. At that time the Lord turned and looked at Peter, and Peter, remembering the Lord's word to him, went outside and wept bitterly (Luke 22:54-62).

After Peter denied the Lord, the Lord could have forgotten about him. However, the Lord did not forget him. On the morning of the Lord's resurrection, an angel said to several women, "Go, tell His disciples and Peter..." (Mark 16:7). Also, the Lord personally told Mary the Magdalene, "Go to My brothers..." (John 20:17). The Lord called His disciples "brothers" and particularly mentioned Peter's name. In this way He captivated Peter.

The Lord Jesus must have possessed some aromatic virtues in His humanity that could attract and captivate people.

Otherwise, there could not have been so many people who would follow Him. Among them, there were even a number of noble women who cared only for the Lord and who simply followed Him continually for three and a half years (Luke 8:1-3). Sometimes when the Lord spoke certain words that were in another realm, the divine and mystical realm, His disciples could not understand or apprehend them because they had not yet entered into that realm. It was not until after the Lord's resurrection, when they had been regenerated, that they understood what the Lord had told them before (John 16:13; cf. 2:22).

Christ expressed His aromatic virtues by which He attracted and captivated people, not by living His human life in the flesh but by living His divine life in resurrection. He was in the flesh, but He did not live by His human life in His flesh; rather, He lived by His divine life in His resurrection. Today, as God-men, by which life do we live? No doubt, we are all in the flesh. Nevertheless, we can get out of the realm of the flesh and enter into resurrection to live by the divine life in resurrection, that is, in the divine and mystical realm.

Today the kind of living we have depends upon the kind of life by which we live in our physical body. We must not live by the human life but by the divine life. Galatians 2:20 says, "It is no longer I who live, but it is Christ who lives in me." This means that we should not live the life of the old "I" but the life of the new "I." Dear brothers, we cannot listen to these detailed points and simply let them go. May the Lord cover me. It is after I have studied these things for several decades that I can be led by the Lord to put them into writing. You need to actually experience these things.

4. To Accomplish His All-inclusive Judicial Redemption

In His full ministry in the first stage of His incarnation, Christ accomplished four great things. First, He brought the infinite God into the finite man; second, He united and mingled the Triune God with the tripartite man; third, He expressed the bountiful God in His rich attributes through His aromatic virtues; and fourth, eventually, He accomplished His all-inclusive judicial redemption. The first two things were concerning His birth, the third thing was concerning His human living, and the fourth thing was concerning His death. After He passed through His human living, He went to die on the cross for the accomplishment of His all-inclusive judicial redemption.

The all-inclusive judicial redemption of Christ is of five aspects. First, He terminated all things of the old creation. Second, He redeemed all the things created by God and fallen in sin (Heb. 2:9; Col. 1:20). Everything belonging to the old creation was terminated by Christ through His death. After this termination, He redeemed back all the things created by God and fallen in sin. Third, He created (conceived) the new man with His divine element. Ephesians 2:15 says that on the cross He created the Jewish believers and the Gentile believers in Himself into one new man. That creation was a conception. Any conception requires an element; without the element, there cannot be a conception. Christ created (conceived) the new man in Himself, indicating that He was the very element for the conceiving of the new man. He conceived in Himself as the element the two peoples into one new man. While the Lord Jesus was dying on the cross, He was creating the new man.

Fourth, when Christ accomplished His all-inclusive judicial redemption, He released His divine life from the shell of His humanity. John 12:24 says that the Lord Jesus was a grain of wheat. Unless the grain of wheat falls into the ground and dies, its outer shell cannot be broken and its life within cannot be released. Christ had the divine life, but it was concealed in the shell of His humanity. Hence, He needed to suffer death on the cross that the shell of His humanity might be broken to release His divine life from His human shell.

Fifth, in accomplishing His all-inclusive judicial death, Christ also laid a foundation for His organic salvation and set up the procedure to attain His ministry in the stage of His inclusion. Christ's judicial redemption is the foundation of His organic salvation. Christ in His full ministry in the second stage of His inclusion requires a procedure, and His judicial redemption is such a procedure to accomplish His ministry in the stage of His inclusion.

LEARNING TO ENTER INTO, TO SPEAK,
AND TO EXPERIENCE

Concerning all the crucial points mentioned above, we need to learn them in a thorough and penetrating way and spend time to study them with much endeavoring. I have spoken on some of these crucial points before, and you have also heard them. Nevertheless, you need to learn to enter into them, to speak them, and to let all of them become your experience.

HOW TO BE A CO-WORKER AND AN ELDER

(2)

OUTLINE

II. To experience and enjoy Christ (to gain Christ—Phil. 3:8) in His full ministry in His three divine and mystical stages:

  B. In the second stage, the stage of His inclusion, from His resurrection to the degradation of the church:

    1. To be begotten as God's firstborn Son:

      a. From eternity past without beginning, Christ was God's only begotten Son:

        1) Possessing only divinity, without humanity.

        2) Not having passed through death into resurrection.

      b. In incarnation the only begotten Son of God became flesh to be a God-man, a man possessing both the divine nature and the human nature.

      c. Through death and resurrection Christ in the flesh as the seed of David was designated to be the firstborn Son of God:

        1) In death His humanity was crucified.

        2) In resurrection His crucified humanity was made alive by the Spirit of His divinity and was uplifted into the sonship of the only begotten Son of God.

        3) Thus, He was begotten by God in His resurrection to be the firstborn Son of God.

    2. To become the life-giving Spirit:

a. First Corinthians 15:45b says, "The last Adam [Christ in the flesh] became a life-giving Spirit."

b. This life-giving Spirit "was not yet" before the resurrection of Christ—the glorification of Christ—John 7:39.

c. Christ, the Son of God as the second of the Divine Trinity, after completing His ministry on the earth, became (was transfigured into) the life-giving Spirit in His resurrection:

  1) This life-giving Spirit is signified by the water that flowed out of the pierced side of Jesus on the cross—John 19:34.

  2) To release the divine life that was confined in the shell of Christ's humanity and to dispense it into His believers, making them the many members which constitute His Body—John 12:24.

d. This life-giving Spirit who is the pneumatic Christ is also called:

  1) The Spirit of life—Rom. 8:2.

  2) The Spirit of Jesus—Acts 16:7.

  3) The Spirit of Christ—Rom. 8:9.

  4) The Spirit of Jesus Christ—Phil. 1:19.

  5) The Lord Spirit—2 Cor. 3:18.

3. To regenerate the believers for His Body— 1 Pet. 1:3:

a. The pneumatic Christ became the life-giving Spirit for the regenerating of the believers, making them the many sons of God born of God with Him in the one universally big delivery:

  1) For the composition of the house of God, even the household of God.

  2) For the constitution of the Body of Christ to be His fullness, His expression and expansion, to consummate the eternal expression and expansion of the processed and consummated Triune God:

        a) All the believers of Christ in this one Spirit have been baptized into the one Body of Christ—1 Cor. 12:13a.

        b) All the believers who are baptized in this one Spirit are given to drink this Spirit—1 Cor. 12:13b.

    b. The Christ in resurrection giving Himself as the all-inclusive life-giving Spirit without measure through His speaking of the words of God—John 3:34.

    c. All the believers in Christ are built up into a dwelling place of God in their spirit indwelt by Him as the Spirit—Eph. 2:22:

        1) Through dispositional sanctification—Rom. 15:16.

        2) Through renewing—Titus 3:5.

        3) Through transformation—2 Cor. 3:18.

        4) Through conformation—Rom. 8:29.

Prayer: O Lord, thank You that You are the Lord who speaks and who gives to us the Spirit, even the unlimited Spirit. We believe that You will speak here tonight and will give us the unlimited Spirit. We are not eloquent, we cannot speak, and we do not know how to receive. Your word has been spoken, but we do not get it; Your Spirit has been poured out here, but we cannot receive. We are indeed utterly pitiful. Nevertheless, Your mercy is rich and Your grace is abounding. We look to You for Your rich mercy and Your abounding grace. Besides this, we have no way. O Lord, we are a group of pitiful ones who gather at Your feet waiting for Your mercy. Amen.

In the preceding message we saw that, as co-workers and elders, we must first know Christ in four particular items. Then after knowing Him, we have to experience and enjoy Him that we may gain Him. But how do we experience, enjoy, and gain Him? We experience, enjoy, and gain Him (Phil. 3:8) according to His full ministry in His three divine and mystical stages, that is, according to all that He has done and is doing in His three stages.

B. In the Second Stage, the Stage of His Inclusion, from His Resurrection to the Degradation of the Church

The first stage of Christ's full ministry was the stage of His incarnation, from His birth through His human living to His death. The second stage is the stage of His inclusion, from His resurrection to the degradation of the church. We need to see why we call it the stage of inclusion. In His first stage He possessed only two elements—divinity and humanity. This was a little more complicated than what He had prior to His incarnation. Before His incarnation, in eternity past, He possessed only one element—divinity. From the time of His incarnation, when He put on human nature, He possessed humanity in addition to His divinity; hence, He had two natures. After His death and resurrection, more elements were added to Him in His resurrection. In His resurrection, the last Adam, Christ in the stage of His incarnation, became the life-giving Spirit. This "becoming" made Him the Christ of inclusion, with the divine element and the human element included in Him, with the element of His death and its effectiveness included in Him, and with the element of His resurrection and its power included in Him. Hence, in the Old Testament there is the type of the holy anointing ointment (Exo. 30:22-25). The holy anointing ointment was not merely oil, which was just one of the ingredients; it was an ointment compounded with many ingredients. The holy anointing ointment typifies the compound, life-giving Spirit whom Christ became in the stage of His inclusion.

This light was hidden from us until 1954 when we saw it clearly through *The Spirit of Christ,* a book written by Andrew Murray. In chapter five of his book, Andrew Murray indicates that in the Spirit of the glorified Jesus today there is not only His human nature but also His death with its effectiveness and His resurrection with its power. In 1954, in Hong Kong, I released a message saying that in the Spirit of the glorified Jesus there are the divine element, the human element, the element of His death with its effectiveness, and the element of His resurrection with its power. All these elements can be likened to the ingredients in a dose which contains a germ-killing element like the effectiveness of death and a life-supplying element like the power of resurrection. The elements contained in the Spirit of Christ are bountiful and all-inclusive.

In the stage of His inclusion Christ accomplished three great things. First, He was begotten as God's firstborn Son; second, He became the life-giving Spirit; and third, He regenerated His believers for His Body. Apparently, these great things are quite simple, but actually they are very complicated.

1. To Be Begotten as God's Firstborn Son

a. From Eternity Past without Beginning, Christ Was God's Only Begotten Son

From eternity past without beginning, Christ was God's only begotten Son. As such, He possessed only divinity and was without humanity, because He had not yet become flesh to pass through death and enter into resurrection. In the Gospel of John the Lord said, "I am the resurrection and the life" (11:25). In eternity past He was already resurrection just as He was life, but He had not yet entered into the experience of resurrection. For example, you may be a professor but still lack the experience of being a professor. The Lord is resurrection, and He has been resurrection from eternity past because He is God, who is resurrection. To be resurrected is to overcome and transcend death, that is, to enter into and come out of death. As the only begotten Son of God, Christ is resurrection from eternity, but then He did not have the experience of resurrection. It was not until after He had accomplished His ministry in the flesh through His death that He entered into resurrection.

b. In Incarnation the Only Begotten Son of God Became Flesh to Be a God-man, a Man Possessing Both the Divine Nature and the Human Nature

In His incarnation the only begotten Son of God became flesh to be a God-man, a man possessing both the divine nature and the human nature.

c. Through Death and Resurrection Christ in the Flesh as the Seed of David Was Designated to Be the Firstborn Son of God

Romans 1:3-4 tells us that through His death and resurrection Christ in the flesh as the seed of David was designated to be the firstborn Son of God. Before His incarnation, Christ, the divine One, was already the Son of God (John 1:18; Rom. 8:3). By incarnation He put on an element, the human flesh, which had nothing to do with divinity; that part of Him needed to be sanctified and uplifted by passing through death and resurrection. By resurrection His human nature was sanctified, uplifted, and transformed. Hence, by resurrection He was designated the Son of God with His humanity (Acts 13:33; Heb. 1:5). His resurrection was His designation. In the upcoming winter training, we will have a further crystallization-study of Romans to see something more concerning Christ's human nature and divine nature and how He was designated to be the firstborn Son of God.

1) In Death His Humanity Was Crucified

In His death Christ's humanity was crucified. When Christ was crucified on the cross, His humanity was crucified there. First Peter 3:18 says, "Christ...on the one hand being put to death in the flesh, but on the other, made alive in the Spirit." Here we can see that when He died, it was His flesh that was crucified. His divinity was not crucified; rather, it became very active. It is not easy for the readers of the Bible to see that when Christ was on the cross, while His flesh was being put to death, His divinity was actively working.

2) In Resurrection His Crucified Humanity Was Made Alive by the Spirit of His Divinity and Was Uplifted into the Sonship of the Only Begotten Son of God

Then, in the resurrection of Christ, His crucified humanity was made alive by the Spirit of His divinity and was uplifted into the sonship of the only begotten Son of God. For example, a grain of wheat falls into the ground and dies. That death causes the shell of the grain to be broken and destroyed, yet at the same time, the life within the grain is made active. The outward shell is broken and dies, but the life within is activated and begins to germinate and grow. This germination, this growth, is resurrection. In *Hymns*, #482 the first two lines of stanza 1 say, "I am crucified with Christ, / And the cross hath set me free"; then the first two lines of stanza 3 say, "This the secret nature hideth, / Harvest grows from buried grain." When a grain of wheat is buried in the ground, is it dying or living? If the grain of wheat were merely dying, no farmer would want to sow any grain. Everyone who sows knows that although a grain dies alone when it is sown, it brings forth thirty grains, sixty grains, and even a hundred grains.

John 12:24 says, "Unless the grain of wheat falls into the ground and dies, it abides alone; but if it dies, it bears much fruit." To bear much fruit is to be made alive, and this takes place at the time of dying. The grain of wheat, on the one hand, is dying, but on the other hand, is being made alive. The same is true with Christ when He was on the cross. Although His humanity, His flesh, as His outer shell, was crucified on the cross, the Spirit as the essence of His divinity was greatly activated so that His crucified humanity might be made alive in resurrection. Not only so, when His humanity was made alive, it was uplifted into the sonship of the only begotten Son of God. In other words, as soon as He was resurrected, His humanity was uplifted into the divine sonship. Thus, He was begotten to be the firstborn Son of God.

3) Thus, He Was Begotten by God in His Resurrection to Be the Firstborn Son of God

The only begotten son is different from the firstborn son. The "only begotten son" means that there is only one son, whereas the "firstborn son" means that there are at least two sons. Those who were begotten with Christ in His resurrection were not just two, but millions. Ephesians 2:5 says that God "made us alive together with Christ," and verse 6 says that He "raised us up together with Him." We were enlivened by being made alive together with Christ, and then we were resurrected together with Him. When He died on the cross, we also died with Him there. While He was dying on the cross, His Spirit of life was making Him alive and also making us alive. Thus, we were made alive with Him and were resurrected with Him. His resurrection was His birth, in which He was begotten to be God's firstborn Son (Acts 13:33). Our resurrection was also our birth, in which we were born to be God's many sons (1 Pet. 1:3). He is God's firstborn Son; we are God's many sons (Rom. 8:29).

2. To Become the Life-giving Spirit

The second great thing accomplished by Christ in the stage of His inclusion was that He became the life-giving Spirit (1 Cor. 15:45b). In His resurrection, not only was He begotten to be the firstborn Son of God, but also as the last Adam in the flesh He became the life-giving Spirit. Christ's being the last Adam means that after Him there is no more Adam. In Christ,

Adam was ended. In resurrection Christ as the last Adam in the flesh became the life-giving Spirit.

a. The Last Adam (Christ in the Flesh) Became a Life-giving Spirit

First Corinthians 15:45b says, "The last Adam [Christ in the flesh] became a life-giving Spirit." First, in His incarnation, Christ became flesh for accomplishing redemption. Then in His resurrection, Christ, the last Adam, became the life-giving Spirit for dispensing life.

b. This Life-giving Spirit "Was Not Yet" before the Resurrection of Christ— the Glorification of Christ

John 7:39 says, "...for the Spirit was not yet, because Jesus had not yet been glorified." In my youth, when I read this portion of the Word, I wondered why "the Spirit was not yet." Had not the Spirit of God already been there for a long time? Does not Genesis 1:2 say that the Spirit of God was moving upon the face of the waters? Then in the Old Testament, in God's relationship with man, the Spirit of Jehovah is mentioned (Judg. 6:34; Isa. 61:1). At the beginning of the New Testament, in the conception of the Lord Jesus, the Holy Spirit came (Matt. 1:18, 20). The *Holy* Spirit in Greek is also "the Spirit, the holy." The word *holy* here indicates that the Spirit can make the common people holy. Therefore, Mary, a common virgin, brought forth a son named Jesus who was called the holy thing (Luke 1:35). Thus, according to the holy Scriptures and the facts, had not the Holy Spirit been there? Why is it that John 7 says that the Spirit was not yet because Jesus had not yet been glorified, that is, had not yet been resurrected?

After many years of study, I became clear that indeed Jesus was glorified when He was resurrected (Luke 24:26). Before He was resurrected, that is, before He was glorified, the Spirit of God was not the life-giving Spirit. Before the resurrection of Christ, the Spirit of God could move upon the face of the waters, could contact people, and could sanctify people, but He could not impart life into people, because He was not yet the life-giving Spirit. The title *the Spirit of life* was not mentioned until Romans 8:2. Therefore, prior to the resurrection of Christ, *the Spirit was not yet* means that there was not yet the life-giving Spirit.

c. Christ Was Transfigured
into the Life-giving Spirit in His Resurrection

Christ, the Son of God as the second of the Divine Trinity, after completing His ministry on the earth, became (was transfigured into) the life-giving Spirit in His resurrection. In the previous stage Christ was a man in the flesh, but after He had entered into resurrection, He was transfigured into a life-giving Spirit.

This life-giving Spirit is signified by the water that flowed out of the pierced side of Jesus on the cross (John 19:34). The four Gospels all give a record of the death of the Lord Jesus, but only John tells us that blood and water flowed out from His pierced side. The blood signifies redemption, and the water signifies life-imparting. Christ as the life-giving Spirit is signified by the water.

Furthermore, through His death on the cross, Christ released the divine life that was confined in the shell of His humanity and dispensed it into His believers to make them the many members which constitute His Body (John 12:24). When Christ was in His flesh, His divine life was held and confined in the shell of His flesh. This can be illustrated by a grain of wheat. Unless the grain of wheat is sown into the ground and dies, the life within the grain is confined within its shell. But when the grain is sown into the ground and dies, the shell of the grain is broken, and the life within is released.

d. This Life-giving Spirit Being the Pneumatic Christ

This life-giving Spirit, who is the pneumatic Christ, is also called the Spirit of life (Rom. 8:2), the Spirit of Jesus (Acts 16:7), the Spirit of Christ (Rom. 8:9), the Spirit of Jesus Christ (Phil. 1:19), and the Lord Spirit (2 Cor. 3:18).

Here, we are speaking about "the pneumatic Christ," not "the spiritual Christ." "The pneumatic Christ" means that Christ is the Spirit. When I first came to the United States,

I began to speak concerning Christ as the Spirit. That stirred up a strong opposition from some in Christianity, and they called me a preacher of heresy. However, up to this day I am still speaking about this, and the more I speak, the more I have to speak. Consequently, they can no longer say that I am preaching heresy, because this is an important truth in the Bible which no one can refute.

Today the truth concerning the pneumatic Christ has spread to many countries in the world, the most evident of which is Russia. The brothers from Russia told me that on the previous Lord's Day they had a joint Lord's table in Moscow with an attendance of over seven hundred people. In that gathering it was purposely arranged not to let the American brothers or the Chinese brothers do anything or say anything. From the beginning to the end the Russian saints served in the entire meeting in every great or small thing. Within a few years after the Lord's recovery spread to Russia in 1991, the Russian saints have grown in life and truth. A brother, after seeing their meeting, said, "They are exactly like all the people in the Lord's recovery." This is truly the Lord's doing.

This pneumatic Christ, who is the Spirit of life, the Spirit of Jesus, the Spirit of Christ, the Spirit of Jesus Christ, and the Lord Spirit, supplies our needs in every way that we may gradually grow in His life and nature unto maturity.

3. To Regenerate the Believers for His Body

The third great thing accomplished by Christ in the stage of His inclusion was that He regenerated the believers for His Body (1 Pet. 1:3).

a. To Regenerate the Believers, Making Them the Many Sons of God

The purpose of Christ's being begotten to be the firstborn Son of God and becoming the life-giving Spirit was to regenerate the believers that they may become the many sons of God, born of God with Him in the one universally big delivery. Therefore, the birth of Christ in resurrection was indeed a big delivery, one delivery giving birth to millions of sons of God. The first One was the firstborn Son, Christ, and the rest were the many sons, all the believers belonging to Christ. This is for the composition of the house of God, even the household of God. This is also for the constitution of the Body of Christ to be His fullness, His expression and expansion, to consummate the eternal expression and expansion of the processed and consummated Triune God.

Concerning the constitution of the Body of Christ, 1 Corinthians 12:13 says that in one Spirit all the believers have been baptized into the one Body of Christ. This one Spirit is Christ Himself. In Him as the one Spirit we all have been baptized into one Body. At the same time, all the believers who were baptized in the one Spirit have been given to drink this Spirit.

To be baptized is to enter into the one Spirit, whereas to drink is to receive the one Spirit into us. The people in the region of the lower course of the Yangtze River in China had the habit of going in the morning to drink tea at the tea house and going at night to bathe by soaking in the pool. In the morning they drank to their full, and at night they soaked in the pool. They said that to soak in the pool was to have "the water enveloping the skin" and to drink to one's full was to have "the skin enveloping the water"; that is, there was water both inside and outside. This should be our condition today since we have been baptized into the Spirit and have been given to drink one Spirit. We have been baptized into Christ as the life-giving Spirit—this is "the Spirit enveloping us." Furthermore, we have been given to drink the Spirit—this is "us enveloping the Spirit." Consequently, we have the Spirit within and without. Thus, in this Spirit, we all become one organic entity—the Body of Christ.

b. Giving the Spirit without Measure

In His resurrection Christ gave Himself as the all-inclusive, life-giving Spirit without measure through His speaking of the words of God (John 3:34). Today people in the Pentecostal movement claim that if you have received the baptism of the Spirit, you must speak in tongues. However, the Bible says that when you receive the words of God and the words of God enter into you, you have the Spirit. In John 6:63 the Lord told us, "The words which I have spoken to you are spirit and are life." Once we receive the words of God into us, these words that are in us become spirit and life. Therefore, when the Lord speaks to us, He gives us life and the Spirit without measure. I truly can testify that the more I receive the Lord's words, the more I am filled with the Spirit, even without measure.

c. All the Believers in Christ
Are Built Up into a Dwelling Place
of God in Their Spirit
Indwelt by Him as the Spirit

Christ regenerated the believers for His Body that all the believers in Christ may be built up into a dwelling place of God in their spirit indwelt by Him as the Spirit (Eph. 2:22). Here, to be built up is to be constituted together. We are being built up into a dwelling place of God in our spirit indwelt by Him as the Spirit. Ultimately, this dwelling place is the New Jerusalem (Rev. 21:3). The New Jerusalem is a city, a large, corporate dwelling place. The dwelling place of a single person is a house; the dwelling place of a multitude is a city. All the believers in Christ will be built up, constituted, that they may be filled with the Spirit, within and without, to become the dwelling place of God. The consummation of such a dwelling place is a large city—the New Jerusalem.

Such a constitution, such a building, is consummated through dispositional sanctification (Rom. 15:16), renewing (Titus 3:5), transformation (2 Cor. 3:18), and conformation (Rom. 8:29). After regenerating us, God sanctifies us in our disposition, renews us in our old creation, and transforms us in our entire being. Not only so, He conforms us to the image of His firstborn Son that all of us may be God's sons in life and nature and, with His firstborn Son, become God's corporate son as God's expression, God's expansion. The New Jerusalem is such a corporate expression, expansion, and enlargement of God. The Bible begins with "In the beginning God..." (Gen. 1:1). At that time, the unique God was "alone." However, at the end, the Bible mentions a city, the New Jerusalem. This city is not simple, requiring the explanation of the Bible with sixty-six books. This is because this city, the New Jerusalem, is the enlarged God. All the sixty-six books of the Bible explain the enlarged God, the New Jerusalem.

THE LORD'S PRESENT MOVE AND NEED

If you learn all these things which we have fellowshipped, I am confident that a great revival will come to us. First, you need to know that Christ is both God and man. Second, you need to know that Christ possesses both divinity and humanity. Third, you need to know that, in His humanity, Christ accomplished His judicial redemption through His death. Fourth, you need to know that, in His divinity, Christ is carrying out His organic salvation in His resurrection. In such an organic salvation, He brought forth the many sons of God, the many brothers of Christ. The many sons of God constitute the house of God as His dwelling place; the many brothers of Christ constitute His members as His Body, the consummation of which is the New Jerusalem.

To be able to speak these things thoroughly and clearly, you need to learn. If you want to know how to be elders and co-workers, you need to know Christ and to experience, enjoy, and gain Him according to all that He has accomplished and is accomplishing in the three stages of His full ministry. Do not continue to speak the old things that have been kept for all these years. People have heard enough of them. Where is the vitality of a vital group? The vitality of a vital group lies in the knowledge, enjoyment, and experience of Christ. You must be able to speak forth thoroughly concerning all the crucial points of Christ's accomplishments in His three stages. You may not be able to do it in a short time, but I hope that you will devote much time and energy to this matter. If you can use a half year's time to learn to speak thoroughly the four items concerning Christ which we need to know particularly, especially the last two items, I believe that a revival will come to you. Do not argue or hold on to your own opinions anymore. We all need to endeavor to get into knowing Christ in a particular way.

In the Memorial Day weekend conference in May 1991, in Anaheim, when I fellowshipped concerning the world situation and the move of the Lord's recovery, I said that in our spreading to Russia we need to pay attention to six things: first, to preach the high gospel; second, to speak the deeper truths; third, to live Christ by His death and resurrection; fourth, to practice the new way; fifth, to practice the one accord; and sixth, to have the full-time training. Accordingly, the brothers in Russia put these six things into practice, resulting in the situation there today. We have been working in Russia for only five years, yet, besides the two big churches raised up in Moscow and St. Petersburg, there are at least thirty-five churches. In other words, there are at least thirty-seven churches in Russia at the present time. In addition to these, there are innumerable denominational groups that have touched the light and truth in the Lord's recovery. They have left the denominations and are desirous of meeting in their respective localities. They are waiting for some among us to go and help them so that they may be established as churches. By the end of this year, there will probably be about fifty churches established in Russia. Such a result is unprecedented in the history of the Lord's recovery.

On the contrary, when I was earnestly speaking concerning the new way in the United States and Taiwan, I incurred some opposition and rebellion. But, where are the opposing and rebellious ones today? The Lord said that we need to know each tree by its own fruit (Luke 6:44). I do not like to criticize, but I want to sound a warning. What the Lord has shown us in His recovery is the best way. We are in the divine and mystical realm seeing the divine and mystical culture, and we have to speak all these things with the divine and mystical language. I hope that you all will relearn. From now on, to be a co-worker or an elder, you have to do this. There is no other way besides this. I hope that you will not hold big meetings with one person speaking and many people listening. This is the way of Christianity which has been practiced for twenty centuries already yet still has not been able to produce what the Lord is after.

Today the need of the Lord's recovery is tremendous. This is the reason that we are endeavoring to expand our training. At the inception of the full-time training in Anaheim in 1989, we had only seventy to eighty people in the first term. Thank the Lord that in this term we have two hundred and thirty-nine people. Furthermore, we are building "Grace Gardens," a community of nineteen houses for lodging our trainees. With ten people in each house, we can house nearly two hundred people. We hope that those who have received the full-time training can be sent out to match the Lord's move today.

HOW TO BE A CO-WORKER AND AN ELDER

(3)

OUTLINE

II. To experience and enjoy Christ (to gain Christ—Phil. 3:8) in His full ministry in His three divine and mystical stages:

  C. In the third stage, the stage of His intensification, from the degradation of the church to the consummation of the New Jerusalem:

    1. To intensify His organic salvation:

      a. For His ministry in the stage of His inclusion, Christ became the life-giving Spirit, the pneumatic Christ, to carry out His organic salvation for the producing of the church and the building up of His Body to consummate the New Jerusalem.

      b. On the way of Christ's ministry in the stage of His inclusion, the church became degraded to frustrate the accomplishment of God's eternal economy.

      c. Hence, Christ as the one life-giving Spirit became the seven Spirits of God—Rev. 1:4; 4:5; 5:6; 3:1:

        1) Not seven individual Spirits.

        2) But the one Spirit who is intensified sevenfold.

        3) To intensify the organic salvation of Christ sevenfold for the building up of the Body

of Christ to consummate God's eternal goal—the New Jerusalem.

2. To produce the overcomers:

   a. Through the degradation of the church nearly all the believers in Christ became defeated in their old man by Satan, sin, the world, and their flesh.

   b. In His seven epistles to the degraded churches, Christ calls the defeated believers to be His overcomers by Himself as the sevenfold intensified Spirit for their experience of His organic salvation in His sevenfold intensification.

3. To consummate the New Jerusalem:

   a. According to the entire revelation of the New Testament, the unique goal of the Christian work should be the New Jerusalem, which is the ultimate goal of God's eternal economy.

   b. The degradation of the church is mainly due to the fact that nearly all the Christian workers are distracted to take many things other than the New Jerusalem as their goal.

   c. Hence, under the degradation of the church, to be overcomers answering the Lord's call, we need to overcome not only the negative things but even more the positive things which replace the New Jerusalem as the goal.

   d. An overcomer's goal should be uniquely and ultimately the goal of God's eternal economy, that is, the New Jerusalem.

Prayer: O Lord, we bow our heads in worship to You, for everything depends upon Your mercy. You will have mercy on whomever You will have mercy. We worship You that in Your recovery, for over seventy years from the past up to the present, You have never stopped Your speaking. You have even given us unprecedented light to see how You carry out Your ministry in three stages in the age of the New Testament. We worship You for these three precious stages of Yours—the stage of Your becoming the flesh, the stage of Your becoming the life-giving Spirit, and the stage of Your becoming the sevenfold intensified Spirit. Thank You for showing us the particular things performed by You in each stage. O Lord, You have been so patient to wait until today for us to be ready in this last age to see Your ministry in these three stages. O Lord, speak a clear word again to us this morning. Furthermore, we pray that You would quiet our heart and open our spirit that we may be pure in heart and poor in spirit to be willing to receive Your word. We pray that You would be with us. Also, we accuse Your enemy, we condemn him, and we bind and destroy him. Amen.

TO KNOW CHRIST PARTICULARLY IN FOUR ASPECTS

Concerning how to be a co-worker and an elder, there are two precious points: first, to know Christ and second, to experience and enjoy Christ in His full ministry in His three divine and mystical stages. To know Christ is very general. Christ is too rich, and His riches are unsearchable, so how can we know Him? In the preceding messages we saw that there are many items of all that Christ is, but there are four of them in particular that we need to know. First, we need to know particularly that He is both God and man. Over forty years ago, a co-worker among us said that Christ was a man until He went to the cross and that after His resurrection, He was no longer a man, because He put off His humanity when He passed through death. It is altogether wrong to say this. The New Testament tells us clearly that after His resurrection, Christ in His ascension is the Son of Man sitting at the right hand of Power (Matt. 26:64). At his martyrdom, Stephen saw Christ as the Son of Man standing at the right hand of God (Acts 7:56).

The Lord also told us personally that, in His coming back, He will be the Son of Man coming on the clouds of heaven (Matt. 26:64). Furthermore, Revelation tells us that Christ is the Son of Man as the High Priest taking care of God's lampstands (1:13). It also shows us that He will come back to reap His harvest as the Son of Man sitting on the cloud (14:14). Not only so, the Gospel of John tells us that in eternity Christ as the ladder is the Son of Man, on whom the angels of God ascend and descend (1:51). This shows us that for eternity Christ will still be the Son of Man. Hence, it is a great heresy either to deny that the Lord Jesus is the Son of Man or to say that He was the Son of Man only until His death.

Second, we need to know particularly that Christ possesses both divinity and humanity. We must know this in order to be able to interpret the New Testament in a logical manner. The book of Hebrews says that, as our great High Priest, Christ can be touched with the feeling of our weaknesses, because He has been tempted in all respects like us (4:15). If He had only divinity without humanity, how could He have been tempted? Who can tempt God? Hence, to deny that Christ possesses both divinity and humanity is unscriptural.

Third, we have to know particularly that in His humanity Christ accomplished His judicial redemption through His death. It is true that Christianity teaches people that Christ accomplished redemption for us. The average people in Christianity, however, cannot say that Christ, in His humanity, accomplished His judicial redemption through His death. In this statement, the modifiers such as "in His humanity," "judicial," and "through His death" are very precious. Such expressions show that we know the redemption of Christ in a deep way.

Fourth, we need to know particularly that in His divinity Christ is carrying out His organic salvation in His resurrection. The judicial redemption has been accomplished, whereas the organic salvation is being carried out. We need to know Christ particularly in the above four points.

TEN GREAT THINGS ACCOMPLISHED BY CHRIST IN HIS FULL MINISTRY IN THREE STAGES

It is not enough merely to know Christ; we still need to

experience and enjoy Him that we may gain Him. To experience, enjoy, and gain Him is not that simple. We can do this only by being in the full ministry of Christ in His three divine and mystical stages as explained in the first three chapters of this book. Actually, what are the things accomplished by Christ in His full ministry in three stages? Simply speaking, in the first stage, the stage of His incarnation, He accomplished four great things. First, He brought God into man; second, He united and mingled God with man; third, He expressed God in His humanity and lived out God's attributes in His human living as His human virtues; and fourth, He accomplished His judicial redemption.

In the second stage of His ministry, the stage of His inclusion, Christ accomplished three great things. First, He was begotten as God's firstborn Son; second, He became the life-giving Spirit; and third, He regenerated the believers for His Body. These three things seem to be simple, but their details are quite complicated. This is similar to our body, which seems simple but is very complicated when it is analyzed and tested in the laboratory.

In the third stage of His ministry, the stage of His intensification, Christ is accomplishing three great things. First, He is intensifying His organic salvation; second, He is producing His overcomers; and third, He is consummating the New Jerusalem. Hence, in summary, in the three stages of His full ministry, Christ accomplishes ten great things. The New Testament simply deals with these ten things. This is the new language expressing a new culture in the Lord's recovery that has never been seen in Christianity.

C. In the Third Stage, the Stage of His Intensification, from the Degradation of the Church to the Consummation of the New Jerusalem

Now we want to see the third stage of Christ's full ministry, the stage of His intensification, from the degradation of the church to the consummation of the New Jerusalem. In his Epistles, especially in 2 Timothy, Paul spoke thoroughly concerning the degradation of the church. He said that all who were in Asia turned away from him (2 Tim. 1:15). This means that the churches established by Paul in Asia turned away from him. The saints in those churches did not forsake Paul himself; rather, they turned away from his New Testament ministry, the apostles' teaching which he preached. All that Paul had preached to them, all that he had nurtured them with, all that he had taught them, and all that he had shown them were completely abandoned by them. The first thing that happened in the degradation of the church was the turning away from the apostles' teaching. If all of us today in the Lord's recovery did not care for the apostles' teaching preached by Brother Watchman Nee and me, the church and the Lord's recovery would become degraded. To remain in the apostles' teaching is a tremendous grace.

Concerning the degradation of the church, Paul went on to say that Alexander the coppersmith did many evil things to him (4:14). Alexander was probably a person who had been quite intimate with Paul, yet in the degradation of the church, he became one who did many evil things to Paul and resisted the apostles' teaching.

In 2 Timothy Paul also charged Timothy to cut straight the word of the truth (2:15), which means to unfold the word of God in its various parts rightly and straightly without distortion, as a carpenter cutting wood perfectly straight without any crookedness. Today some Bible interpreters cut the word of Scripture crookedly. This is also an indication of the degradation of the church. For example, the Bible speaks of the spirit and the soul of man as two distinct parts (1 Thes. 5:23; Heb. 4:12), yet some people distortedly say that the spirit and the soul are identical. Another example is that the Bible says that Christ became the Spirit in His resurrection (1 Cor. 15:45b), yet some insist to say that the Father, the Son, and the Spirit are separate Persons and therefore Christ is not the Spirit. This is not to cut straight the word of the truth.

Paul also said to "pursue...with those who call on the Lord out of a pure heart" (2 Tim. 2:22). Not having a pure heart and not calling on the Lord also indicate the degradation of the church.

Finally, Paul said, "The Lord be with your spirit. Grace be with you" (4:22). If we do not experience the Lord's being with our spirit and therefore lose the presence of grace, that is the degradation of the church. We need to be careful about this. Our highest enjoyment and experience are that our Lord is with our spirit. The Lord, who is the Creator of heaven and earth, the sovereign Lord of all, is with our spirit. This is a tremendous thing. The Lord's being with us is not in our mind or our thoughts; He as the Spirit is with our spirit. Over thirty years ago I came to the United States with a specific burden, that is, to speak concerning the two spirits, the divine Spirit and our human spirit. In those days many American saints said that they never knew that man has a spirit. Thank God, we have been fighting here for thirty-four years, and now it is more common for Christians to refer to the human spirit. Recently, the Lord also has shown us that the secret of experiencing God's organic salvation lies in "the Spirit with our spirit" (Rom. 8:16). Today, Christ is the Spirit, and if we want to experience and enjoy Him, we must be in our spirit. I can testify that, according to my age, without the Spirit's being with my spirit, I could not bear the burden of the Lord's recovery and the churches. Some have advised me not to have so many activities, but I thank and praise the Lord that it is the Lord as the Spirit with me who enables me to have such activities. As soon as I rise from my bed, I say, "O Lord, I rise with You." The moment I touch the floor, I say, "O Lord, not only do I walk by You, but I walk with You. You are holding me while I am walking." If the Lord were not the Spirit but were far away in heaven, what would He have to do with me? Thank the Lord, today the Lord is the Spirit, and we can enjoy Him in the spirit. This is an exceedingly great blessing. To enjoy the Lord's Spirit being in our spirit is to have grace with us. When this is lost, the degradation of the church is present.

1. To Intensify His Organic Salvation

The first thing which Christ is doing in the third stage of His intensification is to intensify His organic salvation. The organic salvation, carried out by Him as the pneumatic Christ in the second stage of His inclusion, is already adequately strong. In the stage of His intensification, however, He intensifies His organic salvation sevenfold.

For His ministry in the stage of His inclusion, Christ became the life-giving Spirit, the pneumatic Christ, to carry out His organic salvation for the producing of the church and the building up of His Body to consummate the New Jerusalem. However, on the way of His ministry in the stage of His inclusion, before He had attained His purpose, the church became degraded; such degradation frustrates the accomplishment of God's eternal economy. Hence, Christ as the one life-giving Spirit was intensified sevenfold to become the seven Spirits of God (Rev. 1:4; 4:5; 5:6; 3:1).

The book of Revelation refers to the seven Spirits of God. The seven Spirits are not seven individual Spirits, but the one Spirit who is intensified sevenfold. This is the proper interpretation of the Word. Christ has become the seven Spirits, not seven separate Spirits but one sevenfold intensified Spirit. This is our interpretation altogether by cutting straight the word of the truth under the divine guidance and revelation. Christ became the sevenfold intensified Spirit in order to intensify the organic salvation of God sevenfold for the building up of the Body of Christ to consummate God's eternal goal, which is the New Jerusalem.

2. To Produce the Overcomers

The second thing which Christ is doing in the third stage of His intensification is to produce the overcomers. By ourselves we cannot become overcomers. Overcomers are produced, not worked out. They are produced by Christ in the third stage of His intensification.

Due to the degradation of the church, nearly all the believers in Christ have become defeated in their old man by Satan, sin, the world, and their flesh. Hence, there is the need to have the overcomers. Today, very few believers are not defeated in their old man by Satan, sin, the world, and their flesh. The majority have been defeated and have become defeated believers. Look at today's Catholicism and Protestantism, in the midst of which are thousands and thousands of believers, but where are the overcomers? There are hardly any. The United

States as the top country of Christianity today has the greatest number of Christians. However, generally speaking, according to the contents of people's conversation and the manner of their dressing and adornment in their workplace, there is simply no way to tell which ones are Christians. Many saints have told me that in their workplace, when people return to work on Monday after the weekend, the contents of their conversation are too filthy for one to hear. How can one possibly tell who are the genuine Christians?

Today's reformed theology teaches people that God has predestinated us, and if we believe, His salvation will be accomplished in us. Hence, once we are saved, whatever we do afterward is all right. We were chosen by God and have believed in Him. From now on we can be at peace without worry; we can go dancing, gambling, or do whatever we like. To some extent, the reformed theologians know the Bible. They see that we were chosen by God in eternity past and that God's selection and calling are forever irrevocable (Rom. 11:28-29). Nevertheless, they neglect the matter of the kingdom, thinking that as long as a person believes, everything is settled; he is eternally saved and will go to heaven after his death. Because of this, after they have been saved, many people live a life of indulging in their lusts.

Because this kind of pitiful situation has been going on for almost two thousand years, the Lord's calling in Revelation for overcomers is still going on today. Christians read the Bible, but they altogether overlook the fact that, in its last book, the Bible uses two long chapters to call for the overcomers seven times, saying that he who overcomes will be rewarded (Rev. 2:7, 11, 17, 26-28; 3:5, 12, 21). Revelation even warns us that if we do not overcome, we will be hurt by the second death (2:11). To be cast into the lake of fire to suffer eternal torment is the second death (20:11-15). Anyone who is genuinely saved will not suffer the second death; they will not be cast into the lake of fire to suffer eternal torment. However, if the believers are defeated in this age, they will be hurt by the lake of fire in the coming age. This is to be hurt by the second death. In his book *The Gospel of God,* Brother Nee pointed out clearly that to be hurt by the second death is to be hurt by the lake of fire.

Certainly, our salvation is eternally secured. Nevertheless, if we do not overcome in this age, one day we will still suffer being hurt by the lake of fire. This is the clear revelation of the Word, yet it is neglected by many Christians. Do we also ignore and are we also indifferent concerning the warning of the Bible and the Lord's call to the overcomers?

Recently, I have often repented and prayed, "Lord, I am in fear and trembling about one thing, that is, that from the past until the present, I am still not an overcomer. Lord, I pray that You would give me a few more years and measure to me another length of time in which I can exercise to become one of Your overcomers." Today we dare not say who are overcomers and who are not. We can only wait for His return when we will stand before His judgment seat, and He will judge whether we have overcome or have been defeated (2 Cor. 5:10; Rom. 14:10). The overcoming ones will enter into the kingdom with Him to reign as kings; the defeated ones will go to the outer darkness to be chastened for one thousand years (Matt. 25:21, 23, 30). Sooner or later we all have to mature. If we do not mature in this age, we will be put into the darkness in the coming age to be chastised so that we may become mature. After the one thousand years, all the believers will have become mature to be the overcomers (Rev. 21:7), who will be qualified to participate in the New Jerusalem. The New Jerusalem in the kingdom age is of a small scale, being constituted only with the overcomers in this age. After the kingdom is over, after the majority of the believers as the defeated ones have suffered chastisement in the darkness, they will have become mature and will be qualified to participate in the New Jerusalem in its consummation. This is the pure revelation of the holy Word.

In His seven epistles to the degraded churches, Christ is calling the defeated believers to be His overcomers by Himself as the sevenfold intensified Spirit for their experience of His organic salvation in His sevenfold intensification. I can testify that this is a reality. It has not been until recent years, especially the last three years, that I know in a deep way what God's organic salvation is. Furthermore, this organic salvation is strengthening me from within. In such a sevenfold

intensified organic salvation, we can become overcomers by
Christ as the sevenfold intensified Spirit.

3. To Consummate the New Jerusalem

The third thing which Christ is doing in the third stage
of His intensification is to consummate the New Jerusalem.
According to the entire revelation of the New Testament, the
unique goal of the Christian work should be the New Jerusalem, which is the ultimate goal of God's eternal economy.
Some preach the gospel with the goal of winning souls. Others
establish seminaries with the goal of teaching theology. Still
others pursue spirituality with the goal of living a spiritual life.
Also, there are others whose goal is to pursue holiness.

In the Lord's recovery, what is our goal? Is it to be people
who are holy? Today among Christians in general, nearly no
one has a proper goal. They pursue being spiritual, being holy,
preaching the gospel to win souls, and establishing seminaries to teach theology and the Bible, yet hardly anyone can
say that they are doing these things with the goal of consummating the New Jerusalem. They have all missed the proper
goal.

In the degradation of the church, on the negative side,
there is the frustration from Satan, sin, the world, and the
flesh. On the other hand, many positive, proper things have
become replacements of God's eternal goal. God has only one
ultimate goal, that is, the New Jerusalem. This is a very clear
and definite matter in the Bible. The Bible with its sixty-six
books opens with "In the beginning God..." In the beginning of
the Bible there was God only and nothing else. At that time
God was only in His one aspect—the triune Father, Son, and
Spirit. Therefore, God referred to Himself as "Us" and "Our."
In Genesis 1:26 God said, "Let us make man in our image,
after our likeness." This indicates that God is three—the
Father, Son, and Spirit—and therefore has the aspect of being
three. Besides this, there was nothing else. At the end of the
Bible, however, we reach the New Jerusalem. Between the
beginning and the end, there is a course of much history with
many ages, including the age of the patriarchs, the age of the
law of the children of Israel, and the age of the grace of the

New Testament, in which many things take place and in which God does a great deal of work. However, regardless of how many ages there are and how much work God does, He has only one goal. In the beginning of the Bible there is one single God, and at the end there is a great, corporate God—the New Jerusalem.

Just as the Bible begins with God, so it ends with God. In the beginning He is a simple God, a God who is triune; at the end a city appears, and that is the corporate God. The New Jerusalem is God's enlargement and expansion, God's expression in eternity, which is the corporate God. Those who participate in the New Jerusalem are all God's children, God's kind, God's species. Today my descendants total only about forty. However, God's children are innumerable. Consider how many are in the New Jerusalem! They all are gods; they all belong to God's species. Hence, the New Jerusalem is the corporate God.

In spite of the fact that the holy Word contains such a clear revelation, most readers of the Bible disregard the New Jerusalem. Some say that the New Jerusalem is "heaven," where Christians will go after their death and where there are the golden street, pearl gates, and jasper wall. Others say that since Revelation is a mysterious book, no one can understand what the New Jerusalem is, so there is no need to pay any attention to it. They feel that since you are not a theologian, you do not have to study it. Today, the majority of Christians disregard the New Jerusalem, the tree of life, and the river of water of life. Instead, they take many other good things as replacements of the New Jerusalem. But the Lord's recovery is not like that. Today we establish the churches, edify the saints, practice the vital groups, and visit people by door-knocking, but our aim, our goal, is for the consummation of the New Jerusalem.

The degradation of the church is mainly due to the fact that nearly all Christian workers have been distracted to take many things other than the New Jerusalem as their goal. Hence, under the degradation of the church, to be overcomers answering the Lord's call, we need to overcome not only the negative things but even more the positive things which replace the New Jerusalem as the goal. We do not want a kind of gospel preaching that is merely for soul-winning. The goal of our preaching the gospel must be the New Jerusalem.

This is why I said that you should not trust in big gospel campaigns. That is not the Lord's way. In creation, in nature, God's ordination for man's multiplication is not by having several hundred births in one delivery nor by having twelve deliveries in one year, but by one delivery with nine months' time, and, in general, one birth in each delivery. This is the law ordained by God. Genesis 1 says that God created man, blessed man, and told man to be fruitful, multiply, and replenish the earth (v. 28). But God's way is to do it slowly. It is by one birth at a time, with only one pregnancy a year, and with each pregnancy lasting nine months before delivery. In this way, after six thousand years, the earth is replenished with human beings. Therefore, we need to preach the gospel according to the principle ordained by God. Do not believe in holding big meetings to preach the gospel; that will not be effective. We have already learned the lesson. Perhaps some will say, "Brother Lee, over forty years ago, didn't you hold big meetings to preach the gospel?" Yes, but I had prepared people to follow up. After the big gospel meetings, I gave all the lists of names to the brothers and sisters for them to visit one by one. Hence, we should no longer have big meetings; we need to practice the vital groups and go out to visit people, one by one, by knocking on their doors. Suppose your church has only two hundred fifty people and all of them practice the vital groups; then by each one begetting one, the next year you will have five hundred. Suppose the Lord's recovery has two hundred fifty thousand members throughout the earth and all practice the vital groups. After one year there will be five hundred thousand and after another year, one million. Apparently, it is slow; actually, it is very fast. The proper way is to practice the vital groups. There is no need to establish seminaries or hold big meetings.

To be overcomers we should take the goal of God's eternal economy, the New Jerusalem, as our unique and ultimate goal. We all need to remember this goal. Our goal is not to help people to be spiritual or to be holy. Rather, we are leading people toward the New Jerusalem to consummate the New Jerusalem. How do we do this? It is by drinking the Spirit and eating Christ for us to receive His rich and fresh supply. Thus, we adorn and consummate the New Jerusalem with God the Father as its golden base, God the Son as its pearl gates, and God the Spirit for its wall of precious stones. It is not according to your will, nor by using your way, nor with you as the element and essence. Rather, it is with God as the essence, Christ as the element, and the Spirit as the way. We need to daily drink the flowing God, the Spirit, as our river of water of life; we need to eat the overcoming Lion-Lamb as the tree of life to be our fresh and rich supply; and we need to take the Triune God as the essence, the element, and the way to build and consummate the New Jerusalem. This is the consummation of the full ministry of Christ.

CHAPTER FOUR

HOW TO FULFILL THE OBLIGATIONS
OF THE CO-WORKERS AND ELDERS

(1)

OUTLINE

I. Beware of:
  A. Ambition:
      1. To fulfill the obligations of a co-worker or an elder, you need to have a pure heart, purified from any form of subtle ambition in intention, purpose, motive, and action in the Lord's recovery.
      2. Never hunting to be the first in any work for the Lord.
      3. As a co-worker, never consider that you are above the elders and never attempt to appoint elders; appointing elders requires maturity in life, being adequately equipped with truth, and not being too young in physical age.
  B. Pride:
      1. Pride is an attribute of our fallen nature by birth.
      2. Even with Paul, the Lord was wary of his exceeding exaltation of himself, so He let him have a thorn in his flesh from Satan—2 Cor. 12:7.
      3. Hence, the apostle Paul taught that a new convert should not be an overseer of the church, lest being blinded with pride he fall into the judgment prepared for the devil—1 Tim. 3:6.

4. Always remember that humility saves you from all kinds of destruction and invites God's grace—James 4:6.

5. Pride makes you a top fool.

6. Rivalry in the Lord's work is not only a sign of ambition but also a sign of pride.

7. Caring for your prestige and neglecting others' dignity are a sign of subtle pride.

8. Referring to your capacity, success, perfection, and virtue is a careless form of pride.

9. Thinking more highly of yourself than you ought to think is another form of pride—Rom. 12:3.

10. Christ in His humanity humbling Himself to wash His disciples' feet gives us a good model of how to humble ourselves for us to escape from pride—John 13:3-5.

11. Arguing about who is greater is an ugly form of pride—Mark 9:34.

12. Wanting to be great and not to be a servant and wanting to be the first and not to be a slave are also a sign of pride—Matt. 20:26-27.

13. Lording it over the members of your church under your shepherding is a strong sign of your pride—1 Pet. 5:3.

14. The apostle Paul's model:

    a. Preaching Christ as the Lord, and himself as the believers' slave for the Lord's sake—2 Cor. 4:5.

    b. Testifying that whoever was weak, he also was weak, and that to the weak he became weak that he might gain the weak—2 Cor. 11:29; 1 Cor. 9:22.

15. To restore a brother, overtaken in some offense, with meekness (a gentle expression of humility) protects us from being tempted also—Gal. 6:1.

16. Self-boasting, self-exaltation, self-glorification, and lusting after vainglory are all ugly and base expressions of pride—Gal. 5:26.

C. Self-justification:
   1. Self-justification indicates condemning of others and exalting of yourself.
   2. The Lord came not to condemn men but to save men by forgiving (forgetting) their sins—John 3:17.
   3. The church is neither a police station arresting people nor a law court judging people, but a home raising up believers, a hospital healing and recovering believers, and a school teaching and edifying believers.

Prayer: O Lord, we praise You that Your abundant mercy is our daily song; we can never exhaust speaking it. Even tonight the fact that we are sitting here is also due to Your abundant mercy. Without Your mercy, we are the most pitiful people. O Lord, have mercy on us, even on every one of us. For more than seventy years You have been caring for and showing mercy to Your recovery, and You have been speaking to us to this day. O Lord, with Your word, give us Your Spirit without measure and pour Him out richly upon us that we may be full of Your word and Your Spirit, that is, full of Your revelation and light. Amen.

THE ADVANCEMENT OF THE DIVINE REVELATION IN THE LORD'S RECOVERY

In the preceding three chapters we saw the full ministry of the Lord. His ministry is neither meager nor fragmentary but full. This Christ, who is unique in human history, did many things on the earth, yet it seems that not many people really know Him. Christianity gives people a very shallow impression by saying merely that Christ is God and the Creator of all things and that one day He became flesh to be the Savior of mankind. Today anyone who has received some education and has studied some world history surely has learned something about Jesus Christ. Some say that only He is the true God, that He created all things, and that He became a man as the Savior to mankind. These things are true, but they are not deep.

Among us, Brother Nee took the lead in loving the Bible and pursuing the truth. I can strongly testify that I followed Brother Nee simply because of these characteristics in him. From the time I was saved, I began to love the Word and seek the truth, so I regularly read spiritual publications. Among the publications which I read, there was one periodical that contained Brother Nee's writings in nearly every issue. When I read his writings, I felt they were quite unique. At that time, it can be said that the Christian writings in all of China were published in that periodical. However, although many had contributed, only a few were unique. Hence, I began to fellowship with Brother Nee by correspondence.

By His sovereign authority, one day the Lord brought me to Brother Nee. The moment I saw him, I was attracted by the way he talked, which was extraordinary. He was only two years older than I. The first time we met was when he came to my hometown. Consider this: his hometown was in Foochow (in the south of China) and mine was in Chefoo, Shantung (in the north of China). Thus, if it were not the Lord's sovereign arrangement, how could we have come together? Afterward, he asked me to work with him, so we worked together for the Lord for a total of eighteen years. More and more I sensed that he was truly a great Bible revolutionary; his interpretation of the Bible was different from others'. Perhaps you will ask if he understood other people's interpretations. Yes, he understood. He had read through the things taught by the church fathers, the things taught by the Lord's seekers after the time of the church fathers and prior to the Nicene Council in A.D. 325, and the things taught by Martin Luther, the mystics, the inner-life people, and the Brethren. He told me all of this history in order to perfect me. He was indeed a good shepherd to me. Because I had received such shepherding, shaping, and perfecting from him, a kind of mutual understanding was developed between him and me. In 1950 we were in Hong Kong together. He came out from mainland China and asked me to go to Hong Kong from Taiwan. We stayed together for one and a half months, from the middle of February to the beginning of April. After that, we separated from each other in Hong Kong with a mutual understanding.

From 1950 to 1996, for forty-six years, I have been devoting much more time and energy to the Word. In 1950, which was the year after I started the work in Taiwan, I had a great determination to build upon the foundation laid by Brother Nee. Thank the Lord that, for forty-six years, nearly every year He has brought me into some new seeing.

In 1951 in Taiwan I put out a monthly paper entitled *The Ministry of the Word*. Whatever I had spoken as messages was published in that paper. That publication lasted for over thirty years. Then from 1960 the Lord began to gradually confirm, both in the environment and in me, that I needed to turn from the Chinese-speaking world to the English-speaking

world, that is, to the United States. The first time I came to
the United States was in 1958. At that time, I was invited to
two places, London in the United Kingdom and Copenhagen
in Denmark, for fellowship and conferences. When I was trav-
eling to those two places, I passed through the United States
in April and stayed until quite close to October before going on
to London. I remained in the United States for four to five
months, during which time I had a deep impression concerning the need of the United States. After a year I came back one
more time. Then at the end of 1961 I came back again. Since
1962 I have settled down in the United States. At the end of
that year I started my work formally in the United States by
holding the first conference, in which I released the series
of messages contained in *The All-inclusive Christ,* based on
Deuteronomy 8:7-9 concerning the good land. Not too many
people attended the meetings. Among them were a few Ameri-
cans who received and responded to the messages.

Then I began to receive invitations to different places.
Since then I have been working in the United States for over
thirty-three years, and the messages that I have released, which
number at least three to four thousand, have been published
in books. In these thirty-three years the Lord has led me to
see and enter into new light every year. I worship Him that in
the last two to three years, ever since I wrote the new hymn
"What miracle! What mystery! / That God and man should
blended be!" my speaking has turned into a higher realm.
I knew that Satan would attack me, and at the same time I
also knew that I needed such an attack, which was a thorn to
my body that I might not become proud. If you have paid
attention, you will notice that since that time my messages
have changed and have become new. I hope that all of you
brothers will be able to catch up with these new messages.

In this year's summer training, for example, we had twelve
messages on the crystallization-study of the Gospel of John,
and in the past we already had fifty-one messages on the
life-study of John. Besides those fifty-one messages, a number
of messages on the Gospel of John have been given on many
other occasions. When we did the crystallization-study, however, the presentation and the style were altogether different.

In my fellowship in the full-time training every Wednesday night, I have a message which I want to share with the trainees concerning Christ as the Son of Man cherishing us in His humanity and Christ as the Son of God nourishing us in His divinity. Ephesians 5 says that Christ cherishes and nourishes the church (v. 29). To cherish is to make people happy and feel pleasant. Suppose when a child is noisy and refuses to eat, the mother tries to amuse him to make him happy—this is cherishing. After the child is happy, the mother puts the food into his mouth—this is nourishing. Christ came as the Son of Man to cherish us, to make us happy, and then as the Son of God He nourishes us so that we may be satisfied in His life.

In John chapters one, three, four, and eight there are illustrations showing us that Christ as the Son of Man came to cherish people and as the Son of God came to nourish people. John 1:29 says, "Behold, the Lamb of God!" He came as the Son of Man to be the Lamb to take away the sin of the world. Verse 32 says, "...the Spirit descending as a dove out of heaven, and He abode upon Him." Here, He is the dove, the Spirit, indicating that He is the Son of God. The Son of Man is for redemption from sins, whereas the Son of God is for life-giving and transformation.

John 3:14 and 15 say, "...Moses lifted up the serpent in the wilderness, so must the Son of Man be lifted up, that every one who believes into Him may have eternal life." He was lifted up as the bronze serpent; this shows that He is the Son of Man. "Every one who believes into Him may have eternal life"—this tells us that He is the Son of God. Verse 34 says, "For He whom God has sent speaks the words of God, for He gives the Spirit not by measure"—this shows that He is the Son of God.

In chapter four the Lord came to the well in Sychar, a city of Samaria, and met a woman who came to draw water. This shows us that He was the Son of Man. However, He could give the woman living water to drink. This One who can give people the living water is the Son of God.

In chapter eight the woman who was caught committing adultery was brought to Jesus (vv. 3-11), who was surely the Son of Man. He stooped down to write on the ground, and when the Pharisees and the scribes persisted in pressing Him to deal with the woman, He stood up and said to them, "He who is without sin among you, let him be the first to throw a stone at her." Eventually, they went out one by one, beginning with the older ones. Afterward, the Lord asked the woman, "Has no one condemned you?" She said, "No one, Lord." And immediately the Lord said, "Neither do I condemn you." That was the Son of Man speaking. Then He said, "Go, and from now on sin no more." Only the Son of God can enable man to sin no more. Later the Lord said, "Unless you believe that I am, you will die in your sins" (v. 24). Undoubtedly, the great "I Am" is the Son of God. This is what it means to study the Gospel of John in the way of crystallization. How different this is from the general study of the Bible!

THE THREE STAGES OF CHRIST
IN THE NEW TESTAMENT

In recent years the Lord has been giving us new messages, and the newest ones are the first three messages given in this international conference of the co-workers and elders. The title of these three messages, "How to Be a Co-worker and an Elder," seems very simple, but the contents are high and profound and not easily comprehended. The first three messages mainly show us the three stages of Christ's ministry. Many in the world know that Jesus Christ came to the earth two thousand years ago, but very few know what He accomplished on the earth. The New Testament, for example, clearly reveals that this Christ, who was God becoming man, was not only God *becoming flesh* but also the last Adam *becoming the life-giving Spirit*. Then Revelation, the last book of the Bible, shows us that He eventually *became the seven Spirits*. The theology of Christianity wrongly teaches people that Christ had only one "becoming," His becoming flesh, and that He did not have a second "becoming," much less a third "becoming." Such teaching is from the backward theology of degraded and deformed Christianity. To this day we still have traces of these mistakes within us. Some are so far off that they say the Lord Jesus became a man for only thirty-three and a half years, and after His death and resurrection He was no longer a man but returned to His original status of being only God. How absurd it is to say this!

The New Testament clearly shows us that our Lord became something three times. First, as God, He became flesh; that is, as the infinite God, He became a finite man. Next, as the last Adam, a man in the flesh, He became the life-giving Spirit. Third, as the life-giving Spirit, the pneumatic Christ, He became the seven Spirits. In the New Testament we see that Christ has these three stages. The majority of Christians have seen only one age, the age of the New Testament; they have not seen that within this one age there are three stages. In the first stage He was the Son of Man in the flesh; this is the stage of His incarnation in the four Gospels. In the second stage He is altogether the Spirit; this is the stage of His inclusion from Acts to Jude, the twenty-two books dealing with the life-giving Spirit. In the third stage the life-giving Spirit has become the seven Spirits, the sevenfold intensified Spirit; this is the stage of His intensification in Revelation. These are Christ's three "becomings" in His three stages. His first becoming is in the stage of His incarnation, His second becoming is in the stage of His inclusion, and His third becoming is in the stage of His intensification. This is the New Testament.

I beg you, co-workers and elders, that from this day you would put aside your past understanding of the New Testament and restudy it with the perspective of these three messages, according to what the brothers from Taiwan are doing. They have learned a secret, that is, they pray-read and study the message outlines, they memorize and recite them, and then they speak them. After going through this kind of exercise, they all can say from deep within that the contents of these messages are the teaching of the New Testament apostles.

Brothers, please put aside everything that you have heard in the past. From today begin anew by learning this new culture and new language. Do not consider that you know everything already. I am afraid that you do not really know. You cannot comprehend these things by just listening to them once, nor can you understand them in nine days. You will need at least nine months, the time required for a child to be born;

this is God's law. Today any kind of learning takes time. I hope that you will devote much time and energy to pray, study, memorize, and speak so that you may enter into the reality of these messages.

Now let us come to the message in this chapter. In the following three messages we want to see how to fulfill the obligations of the co-workers and elders.

<h3 style="text-align:center">I. BEWARE OF:</h3>

To fulfill the obligations of the co-workers and elders, first, we need to beware of certain things. The word *beware* tells us that certain things are against us and are damaging us; hence, we need to be cautious and beware of them.

<h2 style="text-align:center">A. Ambition</h2>

First, we need to beware of ambition. Ambition is something terrible. Of course, everyone has ambition. Anyone who is not ambitious is not human. However, when you come to serve as a co-worker or an elder, you must not come with your ambition. When one becomes a professor, he wants to be a top professor; when one engages in business, he surely wants to operate a top business; and when one opens a bank, he certainly wants to open the largest bank. This is ambition. Even from the time our children are still young, we raise them to have ambition. Without ambition our children will not study well and will not be able to graduate. We teach them that after they graduate from elementary school, they must be ambitious to go to junior high, to senior high, to college, and then to graduate school. In this way ambition is instilled in them. However, to fulfill the obligations of the co-workers and elders, you must not bring in your ambition. Ambition nullifies your obligations as co-workers and elders. Once you have ambition, you are finished.

<h3 style="text-align:center">1. To Fulfill the Obligations of a Co-worker
or an Elder, You Need to Have a Pure Heart</h3>

To fulfill the obligations of a co-worker or an elder, you need to have a pure heart, purified from any form of subtle ambition in intention, purpose, motive, and action in the Lord's recovery. According to my over sixty years of observation, I understand the subtle words uttered by people. Some brothers who may be useful in the church behave outwardly in a humble way, but in their heart they are lifted up. That is subtle ambition, and that is a little fox that prevents them from making progress. The Lord will not give anything more to such a one, because if more is given to him, he will be lifted up. Only those who are humble without ambition can be used by the Lord, can receive gifts from the Lord, and can be entrusted with the Lord's ministry.

2. Never Hunting to Be the First
in Any Work for the Lord

We should never hunt to be the first in any work for the Lord. In the church, sometimes we need to arrange for certain ones to bear certain responsibilities. Those who are not assigned may act outwardly as if they do not care, revealing nothing either in their tone or in their expression, yet inwardly they are depressed and unhappy. This is the insidious work of hidden ambition to compete with others to be the first.

I have a twofold burden for this conference. On the one hand, I want to show you the high vision, which is the contents of the first three messages that include the extract of the entire New Testament. On the other hand, I want to expose the base things in our nature, such as loving or hunting to be first. May we all be enlightened to see our real condition.

3. As a Co-worker, Never Consider
That You Are above the Elders
and Never Attempt to Appoint Elders

As a co-worker, you should never consider that you are above the elders and never attempt to appoint elders; appointing elders requires maturity in life, being adequately equipped with the truth, and not being too young in physical age.

According to the holy Scriptures, apostles are co-workers, and it is the apostles who appoint elders. Therefore, some young co-workers consider themselves apostles above the elders. This kind of consideration is wrong and absurd. In fact, not everyone who is called a co-worker can appoint elders. I know definitely that some co-workers went to certain localities and attempted to appoint elders there but were rejected by the local people. It is neither fitting nor proper for one to attempt to appoint elders simply because he has become a co-worker. To appoint elders requires maturity in life and adequate equipping in truth.

Brother Nee said that one who is an apostle must be able to decide the meaning of doctrines to determine whether a certain truth is according to the holy Scriptures. Both to decide the meaning of doctrines and to appoint elders are not simple matters. They require a person to be adequately equipped and not to be too young in physical age. Suppose a young person who is twenty-six years old appoints a person who is fifty-eight years old to be an elder; this is entirely inappropriate. Therefore, do not think that without you no one can appoint elders. It is better not to appoint any elder than to have a young person doing the appointing. This is a problem which we need to avoid among us.

B. Pride

1. Pride Is an Attribute
of Our Fallen Nature by Birth

To fulfill the obligations of the co-workers and elders, first, we need to beware of ambition, and second, we need to beware of pride. Pride is an attribute of our fallen nature by birth. God has His attributes and we have ours. We are fallen human beings, and as such, the first attribute we have is pride. Who is not proud? Whoever is not proud is good for nothing. In the Lord's work, however, we must try our best to guard against pride.

2. Even with Paul, the Lord Was Wary
of His Exceeding Exaltation of Himself,
So He Let Him Have a Thorn
in His Flesh from Satan

Even with Paul, the Lord was wary of his exceeding exaltation of himself, so He let him have a thorn in his flesh from Satan (2 Cor. 12:7). Concerning the thorn, Paul entreated the Lord three times that it might depart from him. Nevertheless, the Lord said to him, "My grace is sufficient for you" (v. 9). The Lord seemed to be saying, "Paul, I will not remove the thorn, because My grace is sufficient for you. I will give you sufficient grace." Why is it that Paul might be lifted up? It is because no one had ever seen a vision and revelation higher than that seen by Paul. Not only was he born on this earth, but he had also been down to the Paradise in Hades and even had been up to the third heaven. Because the visions and revelations which Paul received were so high, so great, and so many, the Lord, being concerned, permitted a thorn to be given to him in his body.

Now I am also afraid that the visions I have seen may be too high, so I pray daily, "O Lord, I humble myself at Your feet; I am a slave and You are the sovereign Lord. I am truly in fear and trembling, Lord." I am in fear and trembling that I may be lifted up. Sometimes when I receive numerous letters of appreciation, I am also afraid that people may regard me too highly. Therefore, be cautious; do not praise people carelessly. Your praise may damage them.

3. A New Convert Should Not Be an Overseer, Lest Being Blinded with Pride He Fall into the Judgment Prepared for the Devil

Hence, the apostle Paul taught that a new convert should not be an overseer of the church, lest being blinded with pride he fall into the judgment prepared for the devil (1 Tim. 3:6). Here, *new convert,* literally, "newly planted one," denotes a person who has recently received the Lord's life but has not yet grown and developed in it. *Blinded with pride* literally means "beclouded with smoke." Pride here is likened to smoke that beclouds the mind, making it blind. This is a serious matter. When a person is proud, he follows Satan, and consequently he will be judged with him to suffer the judgment prepared by God for him.

4. Always Remember That Humility Saves You from All Kinds of Destruction and Invites God's Grace

Pride means destruction. Once you become proud, your

family is destroyed; once you become proud, your married life is destroyed; once you become proud, your job is destroyed. Always remember that humility saves you from all kinds of destruction and invites God's grace for you (James 4:6). God resists the proud but gives grace to the humble. If you are humble, grace comes. If you are proud, grace goes away; you have hindered grace.

5. *Pride Makes You a Top Fool*

This is my realization of pride. The most foolish person is a proud person, and the most wise person is a humble person. To be proud is to be a top fool.

6. *Rivalry in the Lord's Work Is Not Only a Sign of Ambition but Also a Sign of Pride*

We often are in rivalry with people in the Lord's work. For instance, a certain place began with thirty people meeting together, and now they have reached one hundred thirty. Your locality began with forty people meeting together, but now you have only sixty. Because you cannot stand someone being more successful than you, a heart of rivalry arises within you. In the world, competition brings progress. In the Lord's work, however, there must not be rivalry; rivalry kills. We need to humbly say to the Lord, "O Lord, I am an unprofitable servant. Even though there are more people meeting here with me than with the other brother, I am still an unprofitable servant." In the Gospel of Luke the Lord told us that after a servant of the Lord performs many tasks during the day and comes home in the evening, he still has to say to his Master, "I am an unprofitable slave" (17:10). We all must admit that we are unprofitable servants. We should neither compare ourselves to nor compete with others. If there is an increase in the church where we serve, it is altogether the Lord's mercy.

In my prayer my greatest delight is to praise the Lord for His abundant mercy. He will have mercy on whomever He will have mercy, and He will have compassion on whomever He will have compassion. You have many people in your locality; it is the Lord having mercy on you. I have few people in my place; this may be because I am proud before the Lord, so

I need the Lord's mercy. Always remember His mercy and His blessing. Brother Watchman Nee said that we should not be afraid of making mistakes, but we should be afraid of not having the Lord's blessing. If there is the Lord's blessing, even though we have made a mistake, we are still blessed.

7. Caring for Your Prestige and Neglecting Others' Dignity Are a Sign of Subtle Pride

Caring for your prestige and neglecting others' dignity are a sign of subtle pride. Co-workers and elders who are older are prone to commit the error of caring too much for their prestige. Such a person would often say that he has been working for the Lord for many years, he has established churches in certain places, and he has nourished certain localities. He always cares for his prestige. Everyone has his dignity, so you should not rebuke anyone carelessly. If you do, that means you are displaying your prestige without caring for the other person's dignity. This is also a sign of subtle pride.

8. Referring to Your Capacity, Success, Perfection, and Virtue Is a Careless Form of Pride

Referring to your capacity, success, perfection, and virtue is a careless form of pride. Do not carelessly mention your success, your capacity, your perfection, and your virtue. Instead, always say to the Lord, "Lord, I don't have any capacity nor do I have any success in Your work. Furthermore, I don't have any perfection; all that I have is imperfection. Also, I don't have any virtue; all that I have is failure." This will preserve you from becoming proud.

9. Thinking More Highly of Yourself Than You Ought to Think Is Another Form of Pride

Paul told us that if we desire to live the life of the Body of Christ, we must not think more highly of ourselves than we ought to think (Rom. 12:3). Never measure yourself too highly; measuring yourself lowly is safe. To think more highly of oneself than one ought to think is another form of pride.

10. The Model of Christ

Christ in His humanity humbling Himself to wash His disciples' feet (John 13:3-5) gives us a good model of how to humble ourselves for us to escape from pride.

11. Arguing about Who Is Greater Is an Ugly Form of Pride

In the church, arguing about who is greater (Mark 9:34) is an ugly form of pride.

12. Wanting to Be Great and Not to Be a Servant and Wanting to Be the First and Not to Be a Slave Are Also a Sign of Pride

In His last journey into Jerusalem, the Lord explicitly told His disciples that He would suffer death and then be resurrected. However, the disciples were arguing about who was greater and no one cared for what the Lord said concerning His death and resurrection. The Lord taught them, saying, "Whoever wants to become great among you shall be your servant, and whoever wants to be first among you shall be your slave" (Matt. 20:26-27). Wanting to be great and not to be a servant and wanting to be the first and not to be a slave are also a sign of pride.

13. Lording It over the Members of Your Church under Your Shepherding Is a Strong Sign of Your Pride

Lording it over the members of your church under your shepherding is a strong sign of your pride. The elders often have the problem of feeling that "I am an elder, and you all ought to listen to me." For this reason Peter spoke a strong word, "...the elders among you...nor as lording it over your allotments but by becoming patterns of the flock" (1 Pet. 5:1-3).

14. The Apostle Paul's Model

The apostle Paul preached not only Christ as the Lord but also himself as the believers' slave for the Lord's sake (2 Cor.

4:5). He also testified that whoever was weak, he also was weak, and that to the weak he became weak that he might gain the weak (2 Cor. 11:29; 1 Cor. 9:22). Paul was humble. When someone was weak, he did not have the feeling that only he was strong and the other person was weak. He was a model of our serving the Lord and ministering to people.

15. To Restore a Brother, Overtaken in Some Offense, with Meekness (a Gentle Expression of Humility) Protects Us from Being Tempted Also

Sometimes when you go to restore a certain one, who you are aware has committed a sin, you do not have an attitude of humility and gentleness; rather, you are proud secretly. Consequently, after a few days, you may be tempted also to commit the same sin which he committed. Hence, to restore a brother, overtaken in some offense, with meekness (a gentle expression of humility) protects us from being tempted also (Gal. 6:1).

16. Self-boasting, Self-exaltation, Self-glorification, and Lusting after Vainglory Are All Ugly and Base Expressions of Pride

In addition, we must see that self-boasting, self-exaltation, self-glorification, and lusting after vainglory are all ugly and base expressions of pride (Gal. 5:26).

C. Self-justification

The third thing which the co-workers and elders need to beware of is self-justification, the justifying of oneself.

1. Self-justification Indicates Condemning of Others and Exalting of Yourself

All the self-justified ones always condemn others and exalt themselves.

2. The Lord Came Not to Condemn Men but to Save Men by Forgiving (Forgetting) Their Sins

In John 3:17 the Lord said, "For God did not send the Son

into the world to condemn the world, but that the world might be saved through Him." The Lord came not to condemn men but to save men by forgiving (forgetting) their sins.

3. The Church Is Neither a Police Station Arresting People nor a Law Court Judging People, but a Home Raising Up Believers, a Hospital Healing and Recovering Believers, and a School Teaching and Edifying Believers

The church is not a police station arresting people in order to find out their wrongdoings. The church is neither a law court judging people in order to decide whether or not they are guilty. Rather, the church is a home raising up believers that they may become grown-ups. Furthermore, the church is a hospital healing and recovering believers. When the Lord was on the earth, He ate with tax collectors and sinners, and for this He was criticized by the Pharisees. The Lord told the Pharisees, "Those who are strong have no need of a physician, but those who are ill" (Matt. 9:12). The Lord seemed to be saying to them, "You Pharisees don't need Me. I came as a Physician to open a hospital to receive and heal those who are sick." Moreover, the church is a school teaching and edifying believers.

We co-workers and elders need to carefully consider the above items so that we may avoid these common errors.

CHAPTER FIVE

HOW TO FULFILL THE OBLIGATIONS OF THE CO-WORKERS AND ELDERS

(2)

OUTLINE

I. Beware of:

    D. Not being conformed to the death of Christ—not denying (putting to death) your self, natural man, disposition by birth, flesh, preference, and ambition—Phil. 3:10b; Matt. 16:24; Gal. 2:20; 5:24.

    E. Not walking and having your being strictly according to the mingled spirit—Rom. 8:4.

    F. Not setting your mind on the mingled spirit—Rom. 8:5-6.

    G. Not magnifying Christ by living Him through the bountiful supply of the Spirit of Jesus Christ—Phil. 1:19-21.

    H. Not living with Christ, walking, working, and moving with Him.

    I. Not letting Christ make His home in your heart by your inner man being strengthened by the Father according to His glory with power through His Spirit unto the fullness (expression) of the Triune God—Eph. 3:16-21.

    J. Not working out your own salvation with fear and trembling, for it is God who operates in you both the willing and the working for His good pleasure—Phil. 2:12-13.

In this chapter we want to continue to see the things which we need to beware of in fulfilling the obligations of the co-workers and elders. In the previous chapter we have already covered three things on the negative side which we need to guard against, namely, ambition, pride, and self-justification. In this chapter we want to see that we need to be wary of not doing some positive things. The Bible mentions a great number of positive things. Furthermore, the things mentioned in Brother Nee's books and in my books are the positive things mentioned in the Bible. I have released three to four thousand messages in the United States which cover all these positive things. What we need to beware of is the "not" with regard to these positive things. There are too many "nots" in us. Indeed, the Bible speaks of many positive things, and Brother Nee and I have also been speaking these things for several decades. However, few are those who practice what they have heard, and many are those who do not.

Some may say, "Brother Lee, does this mean that we don't love the Lord?" Many people in the Lord's recovery truly love the Lord and are willing to pay the price; they have also seen the light and the revelation so that they know God's economy and, even more, the Lord's recovery; moreover, they are living the church life in the Lord's recovery and are learning to build up the Body of Christ. For this, I truly worship the Lord. When I observe carefully, however, I realize that the work being carried out by the co-workers and the condition of the churches under the shepherding of the elders are not quite satisfactory to us. We are not satisfied, because we do not practice what we have seen. The many clear revelations which we have seen in the Bible have been released among us and printed in books; also, many hymns have been written. However, I first ask myself frequently whether or not I live according to this light and revelation in the Bible. I admit before the Lord that although He has inspired me to release these messages and compose these hymns of high quality, I do not live closely according to the Lord's revelation and inspiration to me.

The first stanza of *Hymns,* #501 says, "O glorious Christ, Savior mine, / Thou art truly radiance divine; / God infinite, in eternity, / Yet man in time, finite to be." This God infinite in eternity came to be a man finite in time. Where is He being a finite man? He is in us as a finite man. Have we experienced these two lines? The Lord, who is the embodiment of the great God, was the infinite God in eternity, yet today He came into us, human beings who are so small, to be a finite man. Praise the Lord that for us to live is He who is the infinite God, the God in eternity. Although we are finite men in time, He is living within us today. We should learn to apply the truth in this way. Otherwise, even though we have a very good Bible and hymnal, we cannot apply them to us.

The chorus of this hymn says, "Oh! Christ, expression of God, the Great, / Inexhaustible, rich, and sweet! / God mingled with humanity / Lives in me my all to be." We need to learn to apply these words to our daily life.

Stanza 2 says, "The fulness of God dwells in Thee; / Thou dost manifest God's glory; / In flesh Thou hast redemption wrought; / As Spirit, oneness with me sought." These lines are really good, but we should not simply remain in the appreciation of them. We need to ask ourselves whether this is the life we live. God's glory was manifested in Him, but is He manifested in us today? Furthermore, is the Spirit one with me today? Husbands, when you talk to your wife, is Christ one with you? Perhaps in experience you can only say, "In flesh Thou hast redemption wrought," but you cannot say, "As Spirit, oneness with me sought." Hence, although we sing this hymn, we do not have its reality.

Stanza 3 says, "All things of the Father are Thine; / All Thou art in Spirit is mine; / The Spirit makes Thee real to me, / That Thou experienced might be." This is an excellent stanza. All that the Father has, was received by the Son, and all that the Son is, was given to the Spirit. This Spirit comes into our spirit to become our reality so that the all-inclusive Christ may be our experience. Have these words become our experience? Do we have this reality in our living? If we check our condition, we have to say that we are short of such experience.

In a previous chapter we saw that the degradation of the church is due to our not enjoying the Christ who is in our spirit. Second Timothy 4:22 says, "The Lord be with your spirit.

Grace be with you." To overcome today's degraded Christianity, we need to enjoy Christ in our spirit as our portion to be the abounding grace to us. Brothers, we need to bow our heads and confess that we are short of this. Among us, we have the light in the books and the hymns, but we have neglected the practical experience in our living.

Although we may sing a hymn of high quality, the husbands and wives still quarrel. We do not allow the Spirit to make the Lord real to us that the Lord may be experienced by us. Our experience is not "the Spirit makes Thee real to me." Rather, we make our temper and our disposition real to us. When we sing such a hymn, we should sing it with tears, saying to the Lord, "Lord, all things of the Father are Thine; all Thou art in Spirit is mine; the Spirit makes Thee real to me, that Thou experienced might be. Forgive me, Lord, I am not like this. I need Your Spirit to make You real to me that You may become my experience." We need to weep while singing. This is what we should have, even daily. Christianity is poor; the light we have is rich. However, we rarely apply these riches to our daily life. As a result, very little of the riches of Christ are manifested in our living. This is why the burden upon me today is very heavy. I am very happy to have such a meeting. A great number of elders and co-workers in the Lord's recovery around the globe are here. I like to grasp this opportunity to speak a word of love. Brothers, awake! We have the messages and the hymns, but we are short of the practical living.

Stanza 4 of this hymn says, "The Spirit of life causes Thee / By Thy Word to transfer to me. / Thy Spirit touched, Thy word received, / Thy life in me is thus conceived." In our daily life, do we allow the Spirit to cause the Lord to be realized in us through His living word? Do we, moment by moment, touch the Spirit and receive the Lord's word that we may receive the Lord as our supply?

If we compare the poetic words in this hymn with our living, we will find that there is quite a discrepancy. We have such a hymn, but we have very little of the reality of what it speaks. How poor our living is when we compare it with the unsearchable riches of Christ. Paul said that he announced to the Gentiles the unsearchable riches of Christ as the gospel (Eph. 3:8). If we desire to announce to people the unsearchable riches of Christ, we need to experience Him richly in our living. The riches of Christ are unsearchable, but how much reality do we have in us? Therefore, this is a warning; this is something we need to beware of.

D. Not Being Conformed to the Death of Christ

Paul said, "To know Him and the power of His resurrection and the fellowship of His sufferings, being conformed to His death" (Phil. 3:10). To be conformed to Christ's death is to take Christ's death as the mold of one's life. In your living, Christ's death has worked in you to such an extent that you are simply Christ's death. You have been molded into the form of His death; you are simply the form of Christ's death. If a co-worker or an elder comes to the meeting late and still struts to the front and sits on the first row, is this the form of Christ's death? Since you are late, you should be humble and not sit in the front; it is all right to sit in the back. While you are sitting humbly in the back, you should bow your head and pray to the Lord, "Forgive me, Lord, for being late in coming to the meeting." This is the form of Christ's death. As you are sitting there, you are simply the form of Christ's death. Then at an appropriate time, you may stand up and say, "Brothers and sisters, I have always encouraged you to come to the meetings early, even at least five minutes earlier than the scheduled time. Today I feel shameful because I came here five minutes late. I am really ashamed of myself; I am not worthy to sit in front. I will sit here in the back. I beg all of you to forgive me." This is the form of Christ's death. You are simply Christ's death on display. If you are late and still sit on the first row in a haughty manner, that is not the death of Christ; that is a grotesque form of pride.

Likewise, a husband and a wife should not condemn each other; instead, they should always apologize to one another. In this way both the husband and the wife are Christ's death and they live out Christ's death. Whoever sees them will be edified. The Bible tells us that even in disciplining our children we should not provoke them to anger (Eph. 6:4). To discipline our children without provoking them to anger is something that we simply cannot do in our natural man. We can do this only by being conformed to the death of Christ and by living by Him. Unless we are conformed to the death of Christ, all that we have is flesh, pride, and quarrels. If you are not conformed to the death of Christ, this means that you do not deny (put to death) your self, natural man, disposition by birth, flesh, preference, and ambition (Phil. 3:10b; Matt. 16:24; Gal. 2:20; 5:24). This is something we need to beware of.

E. Not Walking Strictly according to the Mingled Spirit

We have the mingled spirit within us. This mingled spirit is the Spirit of God, that is, the Spirit of the Lord, joined and mingled with our spirit as one spirit. The spirit mentioned in Romans 8:4-6 refers to such a mingled spirit. In our living we should beware of not walking and having our being strictly according to the mingled spirit (Rom. 8:4).

F. Not Setting the Mind on the Mingled Spirit

Our mind is always a "strange creature" dominating us. If you cannot go to sleep, it is because of this strange creature. If your heart is troubled and anxious, it is also because of this strange creature. The Scripture says that we should be anxious in nothing, but are we like this? Do we set our mind on the spirit (Rom. 8:5-6)? Do not separate your mind from your spirit; rather, let your spirit become the spirit of your mind (Eph. 4:23). Such a spirit of the mind is a renewing spirit. To be renewed means that we are renewed in the spirit of our mind. When our spirit and our mind are blended together, we can praise without any worry; we can be full of peace without any anxiety; we can be at rest without any agitation. Otherwise, we will have insomnia, worry, anxiety, fanciful thoughts, and wild imaginations. Our mind is like a wild horse. We have to bridle our mind and set it on our spirit so that it may come under the control of our spirit. Brothers and sisters, do we practice setting our mind on the mingled spirit in our daily life?

G. Not Magnifying Christ by Living Him

Furthermore, we need to beware of not magnifying Christ by living Him through the bountiful supply of the Spirit of Jesus Christ (Phil. 1:19-21). *Bountiful supply* is a mystery, and *the Spirit of Jesus Christ* is also a mystery. The Spirit of Jesus Christ is not merely the Spirit of God but also the Spirit of the One who was incarnated, who experienced human life, and who died and resurrected. Such a Spirit of Jesus Christ has a bountiful supply. Do you need patience? He is patience. Do you need calm? He is calm. Whatever you need, He is. He is the bountiful supply.

Often, instead of living Christ, we live ourselves, and instead of magnifying Christ, we belittle Him. We are the servants of Christ, yet we live a life of worrying, of blaming others, of criticizing others, of being unsatisfied, and of murmuring. If we do not live or magnify Christ, how can we serve God and minister to the churches?

Dear brothers and sisters, we should not merely read these items and let them go. We need to check them, item by item, and beware of them. We should not only be wary of ambition, pride, and self-justification, which are not deadly but merely little foxes and small fleas. Much more, we need to beware of the items given in this chapter, all of which are deadly.

What we speak of in this chapter is like the many sicknesses in our body. Today we need to guard against high blood pressure, heart attacks, and many other sicknesses. A flea means nothing. A little fox running around in the garden is also insignificant. However, if our body is entirely sick, that is fatal. Hence, we must beware. If our meetings are not living, fresh, uplifting, or rich, it is mostly because we, the co-workers and elders who are taking the lead, are negligent in these crucial items, not guarding against them.

H. Not Living with Christ

The co-workers and elders also have to beware of not living with Christ, not walking, working, and moving with Him. Many people walk, but not with Christ; they work, but not with Christ; and they move, but not with Christ. Yet they acknowledge that Christ dwells in them. Surely, Christ is dwelling in us, but we often ignore Him. I do not know how many times I have confessed my sins to the Lord, saying, "Lord, I just made a phone call, but I didn't do it with You." The proper thing to do is to say, "Lord, now I am going to make a phone call. I desire that You make this phone call with me and that I make this phone call with You." How beautiful this would be! Sometimes I felt that my wife had a shortcoming in a certain aspect. Then I prayed, "Lord, I want to fellowship with her. Please go with me. If you don't go with me, that means You don't want me to do it; then I won't do it. If You want me to do it, You have to do it with me and I with You." This is my experience of living with Christ in my personal life.

In a newly written hymn there are these two lines: "No longer I alone that live, / But God together lives with me." Our daily life must be "God together lives with me." We cannot just say this in our prayers and sing this in our hymns, and not live together with God day by day. We are too free. If we want to make a phone call, we do it instantly. If we want to write a letter, we do it immediately. We are short of the experience of living with Christ. Often, as soon as I left my seat to go and do something, I had to sit down because I was going alone without the Lord; I had to ask the Lord to forgive me for acting alone. Consider as a Christian how many things you have done by yourself alone and not by you with the Lord. To be a co-worker you have to do everything in the work with the Lord; to be an elder you have to do everything in the eldership with the Lord; even to shepherd the brothers and sisters you have to do everything with the Lord. The Lord is our Chief Shepherd and our great Shepherd. It must be He who is in us urging us to shepherd others. Unless the Lord is doing the shepherding, how can we be shepherds? When we go to visit a brother and the Lord goes with us, that truly makes a difference.

When you go to visit a brother, you must have the Lord going with you. You must not go simply because you have the burden and the willingness to go. If you go in this way, your visiting will be futile. You do not have the Spirit, the life, or the Lord; you are acting alone. Before you go, you must pray to the Lord, "Lord, I pray that You would give me a real burden to visit this brother. I am in fear and trembling before You, Lord. I am afraid of bringing myself there to visit him. Have mercy on me, Lord. If You do not go with me, I will not go. You must go with me. Also, enable me to speak with You, and You must speak with me. Although I am a shepherd to this brother, I want to take You as my Shepherd. Unless You shepherd me, how can I shepherd him?" If you do this, you are one who lives entirely with Christ. You are not in the old creation but in the new creation in resurrection. Hence, when you go, the sensation, the flavor, and the atmosphere that you give him are simply Christ. This is to minister Christ, to dispense Christ. Otherwise, dispensing Christ and ministering Christ become mere terminology that is found in our messages and hymns but is rarely seen in our daily life.

I. Not Letting Christ Make His Home in Our Heart

Furthermore, we need to beware of not letting Christ make His home in our heart by our inner man being strengthened by the Father according to His glory with power through His Spirit unto the fullness (expression) of the Triune God (Eph. 3:16-21). This item is very high. God the Father is strengthening our inner man, which is our spirit, according to His glory with power through His Spirit. When we are strengthened in this way, Christ can make His home in our heart, step by step, smoothly and without hindrance. If we want to let Christ make His home in our heart, we must give Him the room so that He may make home in our mind, emotion, and will. Thus, we become His dwelling place. We are fully occupied by and saturated with Him to become the fullness of the Triune God. Not only are we filled with God but also we become the very fullness of God. The fullness of God is the enlargement of God. In Genesis 1 God was merely God Himself without His fullness, but now He has gained many children. When these children are occupied by Him and let Him make home in every part of their being, they become Him to be His fullness. This fullness is the expression of God. When we meet together, we should express God. When people come to our homes, whatever they see should also be an expression of God.

We have clearly spoken and released many messages on letting Christ make His home in us. But when I observe the condition of the saints in the Lord's recovery, it really makes me sigh. On the one hand, I thank the Lord that He has spread His recovery to many places throughout the world; on the other hand, the true condition of the saints makes me sad because we lack the reality. Today God is confined by us and cannot make His home in us. He is with us in our spirit, but He is frustrated and imprisoned in our spirit, not being allowed to spread out to every part of our heart, including our mind, emotion, and will. We have Him in our spirit but not in our mind, emotion, or will. He is truly frustrated within us.

After Paul spoke concerning the transcending truths in Ephesians chapters one and two, in chapter three he bowed his knees in prayer to the Father that He would grant the saints in Ephesus to be strengthened that they might let Christ make His home in their hearts unto the fullness of God. Today we are short of this among us; this is what makes me sorrowful. On the one hand, I worship and thank the Lord that we love the Lord and know the Lord's way in His recovery. But we still need the Lord's mercy, because our practical living is far off from the things mentioned here.

J. Not Working Out Our Own Salvation

If we beware of the above six "nots," that is, if we are conformed to the death of Christ, walk and have our being strictly according to the mingled spirit, set our mind on the mingled spirit, magnify Christ by living Him through the bountiful supply of the Spirit of Jesus Christ, live, walk, work, and move with Christ, and let Christ make His home in our heart by our inner man being strengthened by the Father according to His glory with power through His Spirit unto the fullness, the expression, of the Triune God, then we can attain this last item, which is the working out of our own salvation.

Philippians 2:12 says, "Work out your own salvation with fear and trembling." When I was young, I could not understand this verse. Martin Luther stressed that we are not saved by works but justified by faith. Why is it that this verse in Philippians 2 says that we need to work out our own salvation with fear and trembling? Later I saw that although justification by faith and God's selection in eternity, stressed in the reformed theology, are right, they are just partial truths. The Bible tells us that although we have received salvation, we still have to live it out practically. When we live out our salvation, that is the working out of our own salvation. We have received God's organic salvation, but when we observe the attitude of the husbands toward the wives and the response of the wives to the husbands, we see that what is being lived out is not salvation. This means that we do not work out our own salvation. Hence, we should be in fear and trembling to work out our salvation. Fear is the inward motive; trembling is the outward attitude. We should be in fear within and trembling without, lest we do not work out our salvation.

In Philippians 2:13 Paul went on to say, "For it is God who operates in you both the willing and the working for His good pleasure." This God is the Triune God, the very God who is Christ and the life-giving Spirit. It is this God who operates in us so that both our willing within and our working without may be according to His good pleasure. This enables us to live out God's salvation. To live out God's salvation in this way requires us to have the previously mentioned items. If we beware of the six aforementioned items, the result is that we will be in fear and trembling to live out the organic salvation which we have received.

I hope that the items mentioned in this chapter will become the practical living in the homes of our brothers and sisters and the practical living in the churches. The work which we do for the Lord must produce this kind of result. If our work does not produce this kind of result, it will not be satisfactory to God or to man. When we were baptized, we entered into the Lord's death and were buried. We have died with Christ, and now it is no longer we who live. This is the attitude which we should have in our living so that we may work out God's salvation.

Chapter Six

HOW TO FULFILL THE OBLIGATIONS
OF THE CO-WORKERS AND ELDERS

(3)

OUTLINE

II. Work with God (1 Cor. 3:9) to carry out His divine building in three aspects for the accomplishment of God's eternal economy:

   A. Establishing and shepherding the churches by the pneumatic Christ, the Christ who is the life-giving Spirit, with His organic salvation.

   B. Building and constituting the Body of Christ by Christ as the sevenfold intensified Spirit with His sevenfold intensified organic salvation.

   C. Adorning and consummating the New Jerusalem with God the Father as its golden base, God the Son as its pearl gates, and God the Spirit for its wall of precious stones, by drinking the Spirit, the flowing Triune God, as the river of water of life and eating Christ, the overcoming Lion-Lamb, as the tree of life with His rich and fresh supply.

Prayer: Our God, our Lord, we truly worship You, extol You, and praise You. You are the God who is forever new; You never grow old and never fade away. May we receive from You the constant and daily renewing. Lord, save us from oldness, from the old creation, from our old "I," from our old man, and from everything old. Lord, may we be like Your apostle Paul, forgetting the things that are behind, leaving everything that is old behind us, and endeavoring to go forward for the prize to which You have called us upward, which is Your dear Self. Thank You for leading us through the past five meetings. In this last meeting we pray that You would give us a simple and clear conclusion, even the best conclusion. Give us the words, the utterance. Amen.

Thank the Lord, in this conference I sense that we have touched the main points and have covered what the Lord wants us to cover. For this we worship Him. In the preceding two chapters we saw that when we are fulfilling our obligations as co-workers and elders, we need to beware of certain things that can frustrate and damage us. In this concluding chapter I have only one clear and simple burden to fellowship with you. This is concerning how to work with God in fulfilling our obligations as co-workers and elders to carry out the divine building.

II. WORK WITH GOD TO CARRY OUT HIS DIVINE BUILDING IN THREE ASPECTS FOR THE ACCOMPLISHMENT OF GOD'S ETERNAL ECONOMY

First, as co-workers and elders, we must have the realization that we are working with God (1 Cor. 3:9). To work with God is not a small thing; it is a divine matter. What does it mean to work with God? To work with God is to carry out His divine building in three aspects—the church, the Body of Christ, and the New Jerusalem. This is God's universal, divine building. All the works of God in the universe are being carried out with this as the center, the line, and the goal for the accomplishment of God's eternal economy.

The goal of the economy of God, which is eternal, is His divine building. This divine building has three aspects: the first aspect is the church, which is easy to understand; the second aspect is the Body of Christ, which is very divine and mysterious and is therefore not easy to understand; and the third aspect is the New Jerusalem, which is even harder to understand. The Bible has been with us for two thousand years, but everyone has been puzzled concerning the New Jerusalem and no one has been able to explain it. Gerhard Tersteegen, a German brother, referred to the New Jerusalem but in an insufficient way. Brother T. Austin-Sparks referred to it more than Tersteegen did, but it was still difficult for people to comprehend.

However, in these seventy years among us in the Lord's recovery, God has given us a thorough interpretation and analysis of the New Jerusalem. In our hymnal we have at least three hymns written in 1963 concerning the New Jerusalem. When you read them, you will notice that the contents are nearly the same as the present light, except that they are not as transparent as what we see today. I do not have to be humble or proud; I am just stating a fact. Concerning the New Jerusalem, all the items and aspects have become clear and have been unfolded before my eyes to such an extent that they are altogether transparent. What is the street of pure gold? What are the pearl gates? And what is the wall of precious stones? The Lord has shown us that these reveal that the basic elements of the city are simply the Triune God: God the Father is the base of pure gold, God the Son is the twelve gates of pearl, and God the Spirit is for the wall of precious stones. The New Jerusalem is built up with these three divine elements.

How is the city sustained? Our life is sustained by our eating and drinking. Eating and drinking are equally important to us. Sometimes we can live without eating for several days, but we cannot stay alive as long without drinking. Likewise, we have a divine drinking, that is, we have to drink the flowing God. Our God is forever new; He is also a flowing God, a God who is always flowing. The Father is the fountain, and when the fountain emerges, it becomes a spring, which is the Son. When the spring flows, it becomes a river, which is the Spirit. Hence, the Triune God is the flowing God with the

Father as the fountain, the Son as the spring, and the Spirit as the river. The Triune God—the Father, the Son, and the Spirit as the fountain, the spring, and the river—gives us to drink of Him daily.

In a preceding chapter we said that in one Spirit we were all baptized into one Body and were all given to drink one Spirit. The Lord Jesus also said, "But whoever drinks of the water that I will give him shall by no means thirst forever; but the water that I will give him will become in him a fountain of water gushing up into eternal life" (John 4:14). This eternal life is the New Jerusalem. In the New Jerusalem there is not only the Triune God as our river of water of life, but there is also the tree of life in the river. The tree of life is the Lion-Lamb. Christ as the redeeming Lamb and the overcoming Lion has dealt with our sin and God's enemy, Satan. This Lion-Lamb as our tree of life has fresh fruits to be our supply. In this way the New Jerusalem is sustained.

A. Establishing and Shepherding the Churches

The three aspects of God's divine building are the church, the Body of Christ, and the New Jerusalem. To work with God, to carry out the divine building of God in its three aspects, we co-workers and elders must first establish and shepherd the churches by the pneumatic Christ, the Christ who is the life-giving Spirit. We must build up the churches by the pneumatic Christ. The building of the church is the ministry of Christ in His second stage. In His first stage there was only the mentioning of the church (Matt. 16:18; 18:17); there was not yet the actual building of the church. In the first stage He accomplished only the judicial redemption to redeem back the chosen people of God to be the material for the building of the church. The church is not built by Him in the ministry of His incarnation; the building of the church is accomplished by the pneumatic Christ as the Spirit in the ministry of His becoming the Spirit.

Hence, we need to establish and shepherd the churches by the pneumatic Christ, who is the life-giving Spirit, with His organic salvation. Our establishing and shepherding the churches should be carried out not only by Christ, who is the life-giving Spirit, but also by our applying His organic salvation.

B. Building and Constituting the Body of Christ

The second aspect of the divine building is the Body of Christ. We need to build and constitute the Body of Christ by Christ as the sevenfold intensified Spirit with His sevenfold intensified organic salvation. This brings us into the third stage of Christ's full ministry, which is the stage of His intensification. The building of the church was not in the first stage, and strictly speaking, it is also not in the second stage, because it was not carried out successfully. In the second stage God was building the church. However, instead of going forward, the church fell backward and degraded into a defeated church. Hence, in Revelation, Christ has become the sevenfold intensified Spirit to build and constitute the Body of Christ in a sevenfold intensified way.

Building may not be organic; a house is a building but it is inorganic. On the other hand, constituting is organic; our body is constituted organically. Building may not be of life, but constituting must be of life. But in the divine and mystical realm, building and constituting are the same thing; we may call it building-constituting. This is our new language. We must build and constitute the Body of Christ with life. To know how to build up the Body of Christ, we must study thoroughly the messages given in chapters two and three. Before we begin the building of the Body of Christ, we must know the church. Therefore, we must begin with the second stage and then enter into the third stage. After we have entered into the third stage, we should not go backward, but we must remain in the third stage to daily experience the sevenfold intensification so that we may build and constitute the Body of Christ by Christ as the sevenfold intensified Spirit with His sevenfold intensified organic salvation.

C. Adorning and Consummating the New Jerusalem

The New Jerusalem is the third aspect of the divine building. We need to adorn and consummate the New Jerusalem with God the Father as its golden base, God the Son as its pearl gates, and God the Spirit for its wall of precious stones, by drinking the Spirit, the flowing Triune God, as the river of water of life and eating Christ, the overcoming Lion-Lamb, as the tree of life with His rich and fresh supply. We have already covered the building and adornment of the New Jerusalem in many previous messages. Revelation 21:2 says that the New Jerusalem was "prepared as a bride adorned for her husband." To "adorn" oneself is to make oneself pretty. This term cannot be used for males; it can be applied only to females. Only females need adornment.

The expressions used in the holy Scriptures are very precious. You have read Revelation a number of times, but have you ever noticed the word *adorned*? I have read the Bible for many years, but it was not until this time when I was writing the message outlines that I found out that the New Jerusalem needs to be not only consummated but also adorned (Rev. 21:19). It is adorned with pure gold, pearls, and precious stones, that is, with the Triune God as the elements.

In 1 Corinthians 3:9 Paul said, "You are God's cultivated land, God's building." Then in verse 10 he went on to say, "According to the grace of God given to me, as a wise master builder I have laid a foundation, and another builds upon it. But let each man take heed how he builds upon it." What Paul meant was: "I have already laid a foundation; no one else needs to lay another foundation. All you have to do is to build upon that which has been laid. But you have to be careful. If you build upon the foundation with wood, grass, and stubble, you are marring God's building. You need to build with gold, silver, and precious stones." For example, here is a building that is to be built with gold, silver, and precious stones. Yet you hang a few pieces of wood on it and put a pile of grass and some stubble on top. This is not to adorn the building but to mar it. First Corinthians 3:17 warns us not to destroy the temple of God. *Destroy* in Greek means "ruin, corrupt, defile, mar." To build with the worthless materials of wood, grass, and stubble is to destroy the temple of God. If anyone destroys the temple of God, God will destroy him. I have not seen anyone who damaged the Body of Christ have a good result. In these seventy years I have seen clearly that those who have damaged the Body of Christ have all suffered serious consequences and were destroyed by God. This is a serious matter.

Today we are here not to destroy the Body of Christ; rather, we are adorning it. I dare not bring my flesh with me to build the New Jerusalem; that is to destroy the New Jerusalem. I dare not bring my opinions, my old "I," my preferences, and my views to build the New Jerusalem. I simply want to be in fear and trembling to adorn the divine building with God the Father as the pure gold, God the Son as the pearl, and God the Spirit for the wall of precious stones. All of us must have this kind of attitude in our living.

How do we sustain such a living? In this building, in the middle of this city, a river of water of life flows out for us to drink and in the river the tree of life grows for us to eat. What we drink and what we eat are the Spirit and Christ, that is, the Triune God. The Spirit is the flowing of the Triune God; Christ is the embodiment of the Triune God. If I eat and drink the Triune God, I am sustained; I have gold, pearl, and precious stones. If I do not eat God or drink the Lord, I do not have gold, pearl, and precious stones; I have only wood, grass, and stubble. This does not mean that only our losing our temper is considered wood, grass, and stubble. Actually, our meekness and even our diligent service may not be the Triune God but wood, grass, and stubble.

In the past there was a large frame in my study in which these words were written: "...he himself will be saved, yet so as through fire" (1 Cor. 3:15). If you build the temple of God with gold, silver, and precious stones, you will receive a reward. However, if you build with wood, grass, and stubble, your work will be consumed, but you yourself will be saved, yet so as through fire. This may be likened to a piece of land that was on fire, and the wood, grass, and stubble upon it were burned. The land itself could not be consumed, yet it went through the burning by fire. I hung that portion of 1 Corinthians on the wall in my home so that I might always be reminded: "Man, be careful; do not try to build the Body of Christ and the New Jerusalem with your nature, disposition, old 'I,' old creation, self, inclination, and preference. If you do, you will destroy the Body of Christ." Whenever we touch the eternal goal of God, the New Jerusalem, we need to be very pure; we must not be careless.

In summary, this message tells us that we need to work with God to carry out His divine building in three aspects—the church, the Body, and the holy city. God's building is first an assembly as the church, then a Body, and finally a city. Strictly speaking, the New Jerusalem is consummated not only by being built but also by being adorned with pure gold as its base, pearl as its gates, and precious stones for its wall. This is God's eternal dwelling place, His eternal enlargement, expansion, and expression.

I hope that you will learn to memorize, recite, and speak these messages. When I was learning of Brother Nee, I never had any gimmicks. I only spoke the way he spoke, and I even used the same expressions that he used. Later, others criticized me, saying that I spoke the same things that Brother Nee did, and that even my gestures in speaking were the same as Brother Nee's. Once a certain pastor ridiculed me, saying, "You know only to imitate Brother Nee's speaking; whatever he speaks, you speak." I said, "That is my glory." Within me I said, "To be frank, even if you try to imitate him, you may not make it." To be able to imitate is blessed; to be able to recite is blessed. Do not try to invent new words yourself. I hope that we all can enter into the reality of these messages.

ABOUT THE AUTHOR

Witness Lee was born in 1905 in northern China and raised in a Christian family. At age 19 he was fully captured for Christ and immediately consecrated himself to preach the gospel for the rest of his life. Early in his service, he met Watchman Nee, a renowned preacher, teacher, and writer. Witness Lee labored together with Watchman Nee under his direction. In 1934 Watchman Nee entrusted Witness Lee with the responsibility for his publication operation, called the Shanghai Gospel Bookroom.

Prior to the Communist takeover in 1949, Witness Lee was sent by Watchman Nee and his other co-workers to Taiwan to ensure that the things delivered to them by the Lord would not be lost. Watchman Nee instructed Witness Lee to continue the former's publishing operation abroad as the Taiwan Gospel Bookroom, which has been publicly recognized as the publisher of Watchman Nee's works outside China. Witness Lee's work in Taiwan manifested the Lord's abundant blessing. From a mere 350 believers, newly fled from the mainland, the churches in Taiwan grew to 20,000 in five years.

In 1962 Witness Lee felt led of the Lord to come to the United States, and he began to minister in Los Angeles. During his 35 years of service in the U.S., he ministered in weekly meetings and weekend conferences, delivering several thousand spoken messages. Much of his speaking has since been published as over 400 titles. Many of these have been translated into over fourteen languages. He gave his last public conference in February 1997 at the age of 91.

He leaves behind a prolific presentation of the truth in the Bible. His major work, *Life-study of the Bible,* comprises over 25,000 pages of commentary on every book of the Bible from the perspective of the believers' enjoyment and experience of God's divine life in Christ through the Holy Spirit. Witness Lee was the chief editor of a new translation of the New Testament into Chinese called the Recovery Version and directed the translation of the same into English. The Recovery Version also appears in a number of other languages. He provided an extensive body of footnotes, outlines, and spiritual cross references. A radio broadcast of his messages can be heard on Christian radio stations in the United States. In 1965 Witness Lee founded Living Stream Ministry, a non-profit corporation, located in Anaheim, California, which officially presents his and Watchman Nee's ministry.

Witness Lee's ministry emphasizes the experience of Christ as life and the practical oneness of the believers as the Body of Christ. Stressing the importance of attending to both these matters, he led the churches under his care to grow in Christian life and function. He was unbending in his conviction that God's goal is not narrow sectarianism but the Body of Christ. In time, believers began to meet simply as the church in their localities in response to this conviction. In recent years a number of new churches have been raised up in Russia and in many European countries.

OTHER BOOKS PUBLISHED BY
Living Stream Ministry

Available at
Christian bookstores, or contact Living Stream Ministry
2431 W. La Palma Ave. • Anaheim, CA 92801
1-800-549-5164 • www.livingstream.com